Merry Birthday!

Love
Joan

11-26-90

THE NATIONAL TRUST &
THE WEST COUNTRY TOURIST BOARD'S

Book of
Afternoon Tea

Edited by Marika Hanbury Tenison
with research by Jackie Gurney
and Warren Davis

DAVID & CHARLES
Newton Abbot London

Country-house tea on the lawn in 1899; the house is Knole, near Seven-oaks, now in the care of the National Trust (*Reproduced by gracious permission of Her Majesty The Queen*)

British Library Cataloguing in Publication Data

The National Trust book of afternoon tea.
 1. Afternoon tea
 I. Hanbury Tenison, Marika
 II. Gurney, Jackie
 III. Book of afternoon tea
 641.5'3   TX736

 ISBN 0-7153-7929-1

© The National Trust 1980

First published 1980
Second impression 1981
Third impression 1983
Fourth impression 1984
Fifth impression 1986
Sixth impression 1986
Seventh impression 1988
Eighth impression 1989

Photoset and printed in Great Britain by
Redwood Burn Limited Trowbridge Wiltshire
for David & Charles Publishers plc
Brunel House   Newton Abbot   Devon

CONTENTS

ACKNOWLEDGEMENTS

The kind help of the following is gratefully acknowledged:

The Royal Archives, Windsor Castle
British Tourist Authority
Brooke Bond Oxo
Ceylon Tea Centre
Floor Advisory Bureau
Jacksons of Piccadilly
Ruskin Spear
Stoke-on-Trent Art Gallery and Museum
The Tea Council
Professor Charles Thomas
Twinings of London
Wolverhampton Art Gallery and Museums
Carol Wright

QUANTITIES AND CONVERSIONS

In all the following recipes the approximate metric equivalents have been given in brackets after the imperial measure eg 1 lb (450 g) plain flour. Although not exact—1 lb in fact equals 453.6 g—these equivalents are accurate enough for practical cookery purposes, as grams and millilitres are so small that plus or minus five makes very little difference.

The metric abbreviations used are: g = gram; kg = kilogram; ml = millilitre. A teaspoon is equivalent in metric terms to 5ml; a tablespoon to 15ml.

AFTERNOON TEA IN BRITAIN

Tea caddy, teapot and tray, all japanned and of nineteenth-century origin (*Wolverhampton Art Gallery and Museums*)

Everything in Britain, says a well-known song, 'stops for tea', and yet how is it that we, a small island in western Europe, have taken as our national drink a beverage that is grown in China, India and Ceylon? Why do the British drink tea rather than coffee, which is favoured throughout Europe and America, and how did it come about that the British invented a meal called 'afternoon tea' which does not exist anywhere else in the world: an elegant meal served from a silver tray and a silver teapot with wafer thin sandwiches of cucumber, egg and cress, dainty cakes and thin pieces of bread and butter with home-made jams; more homely nursery teas with sardine sandwiches, buttered toast and, 'Oh goodie', flapjacks; or a hearty farmhouse tea

7

The Tea Phrensy 1785 (*R. Twining*)

with lardy cakes, savoury scones and lashings of clotted cream on everything?

Last year I had a party of American ladies from Denver, Colorado, staying with me. I fed them four-course lunches and five-course dinners but what impressed them most were my afternoon teas, served in the drawing-room on a table with a lace cloth and utilising my best china. That, to them, was Britain at its best, and Mrs Katie Stapleton who has her own cookery programme on Denver Radio described her British trip and how much she had enjoyed the 'custom of tea, delicious slim sandwiches with the crusts removed, each more delicate than the one before, superb pastries, wonderful shortbread, and two kinds of tea served with milk and sugar or lemon. Very correct and very elegant. It is sad that we Americans never have time or take time for this old British custom!'

So how did this strange meal and the habit of drinking what the traveller John Hanway described in 1756 as being 'pernicious to health, obstructing industry and impoverish-

8

ing the nation', at a time when a pound of the cheapest tea cost about one-third of a skilled worker's weekly wage? It was at this time that tea-caddies came into use, often with a lock. The tea-caddy was jealously guarded by the lady of the house or the housekeeper and the tea very carefully doled out by the teaspoon.

The word 'tea' comes from the Chinese local Amoy dialect word t'e, pronounced 'tay'. In Cantonese it becomes ch'a, pronounced 'chah', so this colloquial word, which the Oxford dictionary terms 'slang', has just as respectable a pedigree as the more proper word. Moreover, the first printed reference to the beverage in English appeared in 1598 and described it as 'chaa'. Tea cultivation and consumption in China and Japan were encouraged by Buddhist priests as a way of reducing intemperance. Even the poet William Cowper wrote of 'the cups that cheer but not inebriate'. The Dutch brought the first tea to Europe about 1610, but it was not until 1658 that the first advertisement for tea appeared in a London newspaper. Samuel Pepys had his first cup in 1660.

Coffee remained the principal drink in Britain until c. 1750, although tea had been coming into the country in great chests from China since the mid-seventeenth century. With the tea came teapots, whose origin lay in the Chinese wine jug, and elegant tea-services known as 'china', the forerunners of the tea-service as we know it today. Paradoxically it was the coffee houses (by the early 18th century there were five hundred of them) which helped to promote the popularity of tea. These establishments were informal meeting places where men could gather together for discussion over a cup of coffee, but tea, chocolate and sherbet were also available. Free instructions on the art of making tea in the home were handed out.

Another strange paradox is that it was from China that the idea of mixing milk with tea came. The first mention of this use of milk appeared in 1655 in a travel book written by a Dutchman who observed the practice in Canton (now Kwangchow) where today the idea would be abhorrent.

The Tea Clipper *Taepeing* (*The Tea Council*)

In 1717 Thomas Twining, founder of the famous tea firm, began to sell tea by weight for the first time, and the habit of tea drinking became more and more popular until by 1750 it had become the principal drink of all classes in Britain. Much of this was due to the East India Company which traded between Britain and the East, bringing tea from China to the six-monthly auction sales in London.

Soon the potteries of England jumped on the bandwagon: Chinese tea-sets were copied, Wedgewood produced Staffordshire creamware in vast quantities and Chelsea, Bow, Derby and Worcester sold more elegant and artistically coloured sets of cups, saucers, milk jugs, sugar bowls, plates and teapots for the use of the upper classes.

The development of the British afternoon tea, however, was not all plain sailing. The Government introduced massive import taxes, thereby creating a blackmarket which often sold tea mixed with 'smouch', ash leaves steeped in copperas (green iron-sulphate crystals) and sheep's dung. Despite these problems and the price of tea, it continued to

10

East-India House, London 1802 (*The Tea Council*)

be the people's drink and since it took the place, for many, of a nip of gin at a time when you could 'get drunk for a penny', the trend was heralded by many to be beneficial.

In America, the imposition of a tax on tea prompted the famous Boston Tea Party in December 1773 which changed the whole course of English and American history, and indirectly led to America becoming a country of coffee rather than tea drinkers.

Tea was naturally brought to Europe by sea, and Clippers came to replace the slower ships of the East India Company. Clipper races became an exciting sport followed by almost everyone, the climax being reached with the Great Tea Race of 1866 in which ships sailed from Foochow in Fukien Province to London in only ninety-nine days.

In 1833 the East India Company's monopoly ended, the political and commercial situation in China looked unfavourable, and ideas for planting tea in India began to take shape. Tea had been discovered in upper Assam in 1823 by a Major Robert Bruce, but the establishment of the Indian tea industry dates from 1834 when a committee was appointed to form a plan for the introduction of cultivation. By the

11

A London tea garden (*Mary Evans Picture Library*)

beginning of the twentieth century India, Ceylon and Java
had become the major tea producing countries in the world.

At home, tea drinking was becoming more than just
liquid refreshment and was developing into a social ritual.
Tea was 'fashionable', its making was taken seriously and
discussed at length, and people were, like Lady Hamilton,
praised for their prowess in being a 'fair tea maker'. Even the
coffee houses began to fade from the scene as tea gardens
blossomed in Vauxhall, Ranelagh, Cuper's and Maryle-
bone Gardens. There couples could stroll in the afternoon or
evening, rich and poor, upper and lower classes mingling
together, and enjoy a good cup of tea with a meal of bread
and butter and cakes. But these garden establishments too
began to fade out; for the rich, tea parties served in the home
were originated by Anna, Duchess of Bedford. They became
à la mode to fill the gap between lunch and dinner, held
around a drawing-room fire in the winter and outside on the

12

Afternoon tea in Kensington Gardens 1900 (*Mary Evans Picture Library*)

lawn under the shade of spreading trees in the summer. Guests were invited to share the repast, and hostesses outdid each other by the array of their cake stands, feminine napkins, table linen, tea-sets and the goodies that were offered to tempt the appetites of those taking part. The Earl of Sandwich some time earlier had invented a composition of two slices of bread with a filling in order to dispel pangs of hunger which assailed him at the gambling tables, and these were refined into the thin, elegant slivers of bread, butter and cucumber which still epitomize British summer-tea-fare today. Small cakes and light sponges were devised and everything was very proper and 'terribly, terribly, nice'.

In lower- and middle-class homes too, tea-time was finding a place, although here the fare was more homely with crusty bread and butter, cheeses, meats and potted spreads, with tea-time forming more of a meal than just an interlude to the day. If they didn't have tea at home, then the middle classes would meet for tea at one of the newly opened ABC tea-rooms or, at a later date, a Lyons Corner House where, for the first time, women could actually go alone and not be classed as prostitutes. The habit of the British tea-

13

Twining's giant teapot. The world's largest teapot beside a small Brown Betty (*R. Twining*)

time was well and truly established.

Today, throughout the homes, tea-shops and hotels of Britain the custom of tea-time continues, with or without the cucumber sandwiches; it remains a feature of any cricket match, croquet competition or fête; it is a 'must' at Henley, Lords and Wimbledon and it remains a meal dear to the heart of all Englishmen.

Marika Hanbury Tenison
Maidenwell, Cornwall
1979

THE ART OF MAKING TEA

Everyone has their own way of making tea and some take the process much more seriously than others. As a basic guideline, use a good quality tea and allow a spoonful for each person and one extra 'for the pot'. Keep the tea fresh by storing it in an airtight container or tin caddy. Fresh water should always be used for making tea and the softer it is the better the tea will be. Do not use stale water that has already boiled from your kettle. Bring the fresh water to a fast boil. Warm the teapot with hot water and take it to the boiling kettle rather than the other way round. Pour the water onto the leaves as soon as it reaches boiling point, allow the tea to infuse for five minutes and then stir once before pouring out through a strainer.

Milk can be put in before the tea is poured or after it but the first method ensures a better mixing of the tea and milk. Top up the teapot with boiling water when it is half empty.

The kinds of tea to use

'Not for all the tea in China' we say as a measure of great wealth; yet most tea drunk in Britain today is Indian or Ceylonese. Certainly China first introduced the idea of tea drinking, possibly as many as 5,000 years ago, and had a monopoly on the early tea trade. But when the nineteenth-century British colonists of India discovered the tea-plant, *Camellia Sinensis*, growing wild in Assam it did not take them long to realise its commercial potential. As a result tea production was developed in India on a large scale, out-pacing

Samples of teas for sale in London Tea Auction and also for sale to house-
wives were evaluated and made up in this Brook Bond saleroom over fifty
years ago (*Brook Bond Oxo*)

the more traditional growing methods practised in China.
Also the British public gradually came to prefer the stronger
sappy-tasting Indian tea, and interest in the more delicate
China teas dwindled.

In those early days there was very little blended tea for
sale. The different sorts of tea came direct from their garden
of origin to the tea merchants in London who, in turn,
despatched the tea to the grocers in cases. The tea was then
weighed out, twisted into little spools of paper and sold to
the public. What blending there was became the preserve of
the grocer who began to know the qualities and seasonal
fluctuations of the various tea gardens; or it was done by the
customer himself. As a special favour, the grocer would
blend a tea to an individual customer's liking, a personal
service that has produced teas named after their patrons
such as Lady Londonderry, Earl Grey and the Marquess of
Queensberry.

Today nearly all the 440 million pounds of tea we drink a

year is blended, with supplies coming from Africa, South America, Turkey and the USSR as well as from India, Ceylon and Indonesia. China and Taiwan supply only 3% of our needs.

Importers of tea, like importers of wine, use tasters to maintain standards and value for money. Tea tasting is a serious business and takes years of training; like good wine tasters a good taster of tea will have a 'nose' for flavour even though he may have to taste as many as two or three hundred teas in the course of a day.

With all this time, care and skill going into the daily cuppa, it is a pity that most people buy one brand of tea and stick to it. A connoisseur might choose from the following:

Indian and Indian-type teas

Assam A strong tea with a distinct malty flavour that should be served with milk and not with lemon.
Darjeeling Regarded as the finest and most distinctive of Indian teas this large leaf variety has a delicate muscatel flavour.
Mysore A mild, light coloured tea with a clean fruity flavour.
Ceylon A medium strength tea with a mellow, nutty flavour; it becomes creamy-brown in colour when milk is added.
Kenya Similar in type to Ceylon tea, Kenya is often used for blending.
English Breakfast Made from the small leaf teas of India and Ceylon, it makes a rich, strong brew.

China teas

Keemun One of the most popular China teas, it is mellow and smooth with a pale straw colour.
Ching Wo A delicate, slightly scented tea similar in type to Keemun, it is best drunk with a slice of lemon.
Ichang A dark brown tea which bears a resemblance to Indian teas.
Bohea A black tea from the north of China.
Lapsang Souchong A large leafed tea with a pungent, smokey or tarry flavour. Best served with lemon rather than milk.

Sir John Gay and his sisters c1720 (*The Tea Council*)

Fancy teas

Scented China teas These are very delicate teas, scented by mixing in a small proportion of pleasant smelling leaves of various sorts. Scented Orange Pekoe contains orange leaves; Jasmine contains jasmine blossom; and you might come across the old-fashioned Cowslip Hyson.

Natural flavoured China teas Old Hyson and Gunpowder are two varieties of green tea, each with its own slightly bitter flavour.

Oolong A delicate and soft peach-like taste comes from this tea which is grown, ideally, in the shade of fruit trees.

Earl Grey's An unusual blend of large China and Darjeeling teas brought back from China by the 2nd Earl Grey in 1830. It is delicately scented with oil of Bergamot which gives it a mild flavour.

Lady Londonderry's A blend of Ceylon, India and Formosa (Taiwan) teas used by London's famous social and political hostess during the first half of this century.

Lemon tea A blend of Ceylon teas mixed with lemon peel and scented with lemon essence. It should be served either hot or iced, without milk.

Russian tea A long leafed tea grown in the foothills of the Caucasian mountains near the border between Russia and Turkey. It is similar in character to China tea and is best drunk with a slice of lemon.

Because of the high cost of tea, the ever inventive British soon produced a number of alternative 'teas' made from home-grown plants. Indeed, many of the old medieval herbal and medicinal infusions became known as 'teas', causing a degree of confusion. Not all were suitable as substitutes for the real thing but here are a few recipes of the kind of beverages the impoverished ladies of Cranford might have sipped when making economies.

Hyssop Tea The flowers and leaves are used. Pour boiling water over them (a handful to 2 pints, 1.25 litres) infuse for 20 minutes. Sweetened with honey, it was considered good for chest coughs.

Raspberry-leaf Tea The ordinary leaves of the raspberry canes from late spring to full summer should be gathered and used (fresh, if possible). Infuse in boiling water and drink freely with milk and sugar. It also makes a good drink with lemon and sugar. It is well-known as particularly good during the later months of pregnancy.

Blackcurrant Tea The berries made into a thick syrup, sweetened with honey, are excellent for hoarseness of the throat or to loosen a cold on the chest. For the latter the tea is drunk hot at bedtime.

Blackcurrant Leaves The leaves, gathered in early summer and dried and rubbed, made a good ordinary tea, and was used by pensioners to augment their allowance of 'India blend'.

Blackberry Leaves Dry and roll the small 'tips' of the runners. When making 'substitute teas' the blackberry is chosen to give a good colour.

Household Hints

Tea-leaves had a number of uses in pre-detergent and pre-silicone households: They were sprinkled over carpets to help collect and fix dust; kept for several days, infused with boiling water, then strained and used to polish mirrors, windows, glasses, varnished woods; boiled up in fish pans, tea-leaves helped to remove the smell of fish.

Tablecloths and other linen stained by tea should be soaked in a mixture of borax and water.

THE TRAPPINGS OF THE TEA TABLE

Have you ever wondered why the Chinese willow pattern has found its way into countless English homes? Its popularity, particularly for tea-sets, can be traced to the vogue for Chinoiserie promoted by the trading of the East India Company. As well as importing tea, the merchants shipped over the necessary tea-drinking utensils; which was just as well as few British people had any idea what to do with the precious dried leaves when they first arrived.

The first teapots to make their appearance were the red or brown wares of Yi-Hsing near Shanghai. These were highly regarded for their tea-making qualities, just as the humble old brown teapot is today. Later the styles and designs became more lavish, with porcelain as the prized material.

Only a handful of English-made ceramic teapots can be dated before 1740; but after that date home production flourished, coinciding with the reduction of the tea duties. Many of the new wares were direct copies of the Chinese imports or the Dutch delft. Others featured the newly developed salt-glaze and were decorated to simulate marble, tortoise-shell, agate, or silver. Technical improvements meant that the shape of the utensils could be more ambitious, and manufacturers went overboard creating square, hexagonal and octagonal teapots, teapots shaped like animals or houses or even Admiral Vernon's flagship at Portobello. Later came enamel painting which enabled the pots to be garlanded with colourful flowers, bands and portraits.

Simultaneous with the heyday of salt-glaze was the rise of English soft-paste porcelain, a glassy material quite dif-

Teapot moulded in the form of a ship to commemorate the victory at Port-obello by Admiral Vernon of Staffordshire c1740 (*Stoke-on-Trent Art Gallery and Museum*)

ferent from the hard-paste porcelain of China. Factories at Worcester, Derby, Chelsea and Bow began to turn out the most delicate of tea-wares to meet a new demand—that of the elegant drawing room tea-party. Hitherto there had been teapots, cups and saucers but etiquette had not insisted that they should match. By the middle of the eighteenth century, a fashionable tea-table could only be enhanced by an equally fashionable tea-service and a hostess well versed in the art of dignified conversation.

22

A painting of Dr Johnson
and his cronies using a
silver teapot, by A. J.
Ruskin Spear, ARA

A tea-service of this period generally comprised: teapot
and cover, coffee pot and cover, sugar bowl, stand and
cover, twelve tea-bowls or cups and twelve saucers, six
coffee cups, milk jug and cover, slop bowl, spoon tray, teapot
stand and tea canisters. Large bread and butter plates were
added a little later but tea-plates as we know them were a
mid-Victorian addition.

The use of tea-bowls in the Chinese fashion persisted until
the early nineteenth century. These bowls were often accom-
panied by deep-sided saucers from which a 'dish of tea'
could be drunk without the stigma of bad manners.

In Russia a custom startling to strangers was that men drank tea in glasses and women in china cups. Alexandre Dumas gave the legend behind this custom in his *Dictionary of Cuisine*: 'It seems that teacups were first made at Kronstadt, and the bottom was decorated with a view of that city. When a teahouse proprietor stinted on the tea, this picture could be seen clearly, and the customer would say to him, "I can see Kronstadt." Since the proprietor could not deny this, he was caught in *flagrante delicto*. It became customary, then, for tea to be served in teahouses in glasses, at the bottom of which there was nothing to see, let alone Kronstadt!'

Silverware had been in use on the tea-table since the introduction of tea to Britain; the first silver teapots were clearly modelled on the lines of a coffee pot. By the eighteenth century, the designs featured on teapots were extremely elaborate and elegant silver kettles, often complete with stands and heating lamps, formed part of the tea-time equipage. Silver caddy spoons would take on the shape of a shell, a bunch of grapes or even a jockey's cap.

Such refinement extended to the making of the tea itself. The mistress of the house would be responsible for blending the tea to her guests' satisfaction, choosing from a number of tea-canisters or caddies. At the very least she would have had one caddy for green tea and one for black; or she might have preferred to use a wooden rectangular box housing two canisters and a glass mixing bowl. When not in use, the tea-caddies (so called after the Malay word 'kati', a weight equivalent to 1½ lb) would be kept under lock and key. With tea at such a price, pilfering had to be discouraged, although many wily servants made quite a trade out of drying the used tea leaves and selling them second-hand.

The name of Wedgwood overshadowed all others when it came to tea-ware; indeed he took teapot design so seriously that he always sensibly cleared a new idea with his wife. Wedgwood was famous for creamware (a fine white earthenware), black basalt, and jasper adorned with white cameo; and he popularised styles that were to find a host of enthusiastic imitators in years to come. New Hall was another big name in the manufacture of tea-ware, concentrating almost exclusively on true porcelain (hard paste), until the introduction of bone china which has held sway on the tea-table for the last century and a half.

DRAWING-ROOM TEAS

Tea served in the drawing-room should, above all, be elegant. Sandwiches should be small, individual cakes should be dainty and both napkins and forks should be provided. Tea is usually brought into the drawing-room on a tray covered with an embroidered tray cloth and is then laid out on a small table also covered with a cloth. Both China and Indian tea should be offered, hot water should be at hand and both milk and lemon provided. The hostess should pour the tea herself but the food can be handed round by either a maid or one of the guests.

Tea in the garden is a comparably elegant occasion. In hot weather, iced tea as well as hot China and Indian tea can be provided and this can be easily made by pouring the hot tea into a heat-proof glass well filled with ice cubes. An alternative method of making cold tea is to put the tea leaves into cold water and leave overnight. Strain off the liquid the next morning and a beautifully clear, fragrant tea basis remains. An ounce of tea should be used for each pint of cold water. A sprig of mint or a slice of lemon should be added to the iced tea and milk should never be used.

Sandwiches

There is all the difference in the world between the best and more mundane sandwiches and although the best ones take some time and trouble to prepare the effort is well rewarded. Use day old bread and cut it wafer thin with a good sharp knife—do not use commercially sliced bread. Remove the crusts after the sandwiches have been filled.

Tea-time in the 1890s (*Mary Evans Picture Library*)

Cucumber Sandwiches—1

An all time favourite of the British tea ritual that goes as well with tea on a cloth served under the spreading trees of a manicured lawn as it does with an elegant spread in front of a glowing fire in the drawing room.

Thinly cut white or brown
   bread
Softened butter
Cucumber
1 teaspoon vinegar
Salt and white pepper

Peel the cucumber and cut it into transparently thin slices (this can be done on a *mandoline* or through the slicing side of a grater). Place the slices on a plate, sprinkle them with some vinegar and then some salt. Leave them to stand for a good 30 minutes and then drain in a sieve to remove excess liquid.

    Butter the slices of bread. Cover a slice of bread with two layers of the sliced cucumber, top with another slice of bread and press firmly together. Remove crusts and cut each sandwich into three fingers. Pile neatly on a serving dish and cover with a slightly dampened cloth until required.

27

Cucumber Sandwiches—II

Very thinly cut slices of white
  bread
Softened butter
Cucumber
Salt and white pepper

Spread the slices of bread evenly with softened butter. Peel the cucumber, cut into half lengthwise and remove the seeds. Grate the flesh through the coarse blades of a grater. Place the grated cucumber in a sieve and press it firmly to remove excess moisture.

Spread the grated cucumber on slices of buttered bread, season with salt and pepper, top with a second slice of bread and press firmly together. Cut off crusts and cut each sandwich into three fingers. Stack sandwiches neatly on a serving plate and cover with a slightly dampened cloth until required.

Egg and Cress Sandwiches

Slices of thinly cut white or
  brown bread
1 hard boiled egg
1 oz (25 g) softened butter
Salt and white pepper
Cress

Remove egg shell and finely chop the white and yolk of the egg. Combine egg and softened butter in a bowl, season with salt and pepper and mix with a fork to obtain a soft, creamy mixture without destroying the texture of the chopped egg.

Spread the egg and butter mixture on thin slices of bread. Top with a generous layer of cress, cover with a second slice of bread and press firmly together. Remove crusts and cut each sandwich into three fingers. Pile neatly on a serving plate and cover with a slightly dampened cloth until required.

Marmite and Cress Sandwiches

Thinly cut slices of brown or
  white bread
Softened butter
Marmite
Cress

28

Remove stalks from the cress and coarsely chop the leaves. Spread thinly cut slices of bread with softened butter and then with a thin skim of Marmite. Top with a layer of watercress leaves and cover with a second slice of buttered bread. Press firmly together, remove crusts and cut each sandwich into three fingers. Stack neatly on a serving plate and cover with a slightly dampened cloth until required.

Tomato Sandwiches

Thinly cut slices of brown or
    white bread
Softened butter
Tomatoes
Salt and white pepper

Butter slices of thinly cut bread. Cover tomatoes with boiling water, leave to stand for 2 minutes, drain off water and slide off tomato skins. Thinly slice tomatoes discarding the slice at the stalk end. Arrange slices of tomato on slices of buttered bread and season with salt and pepper. Cover with second slices of buttered bread and press firmly together. Remove crusts and cut sandwiches into three fingers. Stack sandwiches neatly on a serving plate, cover with a slightly dampened cloth until required.

See also recipes for potted meat and fish paste on page 60 for further sandwiches.

Cinnamon Toast

Thin slices of white bread
1½ oz (40 g) softened, unsal-
    ted, butter
5 tablespoons icing sugar
1 teaspoon cinnamon

Combine the butter, sugar and cinnamon and beat with a wooden spoon until smooth. Spread the mixture on thin slices of white bread with the crusts removed. Cut the slices of bread into 2in (5 cm) wide fingers, place on a baking sheet and bake in a hot oven (400°F, 205°C; Gas Mark 6) for about 8 minutes.

Hot Buttered Toast

Medium cut slices of white bread
Softened butter

Toast bread until golden—*then* cut off crusts and spread generously with softened butter. Cut each slice into three fingers, place three fingers of toast on a plate covered with a large white damask napkin opened out. Place next three fingers across the first three and continue piling up the rest of the buttered fingers. Pull up the sides of the napkin over the toast to keep the slices warm until they are to be served. Serve with jam, Gentleman's Relish or potted meat or fish.

Almond Shortbread

Original shortbread was a Scottish biscuit but now popular throughout Britain.

5 oz (150 g) plain flour
1 oz (25 g) ground rice
2 oz (50 g) caster sugar
4 oz (125 g) butter
1½ oz (40 g) flaked almonds
Pinch salt

Combine flour, ground rice, sugar and salt in a bowl and mix well. Add the butter taken straight from the refrigerator and grated into flakes through the coarse blades of a grater. Rub the butter into the other ingredients using the fingertips until the mixture resembles fine breadcrumbs.

Press the mixture firmly into a 7in (18cm) sandwich tin patting it down until flat. Prick the top with a fork and cut through with a knife into eight even slices. Sprinkle over the flaked almonds, cover with a circle of greaseproof paper and chill in the refrigerator for 1 hour before baking.

Bake in a slow oven (300°F, 150°C; Gas Mark 2) for 1 hour; remove the greaseproof paper for the last 15 minutes of baking time. Cool in the tin, turn onto a wire rack and break into pieces when cold. The pieces of shortbread can be dusted with sugar before serving.

Devonshire Biscuits

8 oz (225 g) plain flour
4 oz (125 g) butter
4 oz (125 g) caster sugar
1 oz (25 g) ground almonds
2 egg yolks
5 fl oz (125 ml) milk (optional)

Sift the flour and rub in the butter; add the sugar and ground almonds. Mix to a stiff paste with the egg yolks, adding milk if necessary.

Roll the dough out, ¼in (6mm) thick, and cut into 2½in (6cm) rounds. Set on greased baking trays, prick and bake in a moderate oven (350°F, 180°C; Gas Mark 4) for 15 minutes.

Devon Flats

1 lb (450 g) plain flour
½ pt (250 ml) Devonshire cream
8 oz (225 g) caster sugar
1 egg
Milk

Sift the flour. Mix into the cream and add the sugar, beaten egg and enough milk to give a smooth, stiff dough.

Roll the mixture out very thinly and cut into 2in (5cm) rounds. Set on greased baking trays and bake in a hot oven (425°F, 220°C; Gas Mark 7) for 10 minutes.

Crumpets or Pikelets

A crumpet is a round flat sweet scone with holes in it. The traditional crumpet rings are 3½in (9cm) wide and 1in (2½cm) deep.

1¼ lb (575 g) flour   2¼ cups.
½ oz (15 g) yeast   2tsp.
1 pt (500 ml) warm water   20 oz
1 oz (25 g) salt

Dissolve the creamed yeast in a little of the warm water; sift the flour and salt and mix in the remaining water. Add the creamed yeast to the mixture and cover with a cloth; keep in a warm place until the dough is well risen.

Thin the dough to a batter consistency with a little warm water, and leave for 5 minutes. Bake in greased crumpet rings on a hot plate or griddle, filling the rings halfway up with batter and turning when dry on top and slightly browned underneath; remove the crumpet rings.

It is advisable to test one crumpet first; if the batter is too thick the holes will not form and more warm water should be added.

31

Sweet Scones

These scones may be made with plain flour rather than self-raising in which case 1 oz (25 g) baking powder or 1 teaspoon bicarbonate of soda and 2 teaspoons cream of tartar should be added to 1 lb (450 g) flour; a little more milk may also be necessary. Serve hot or cold, with butter and jam.

1 lb (450 g) self-raising flour
1 teaspoon salt
4 oz (125 g) butter
4 oz (125 g) sugar
2 eggs
5 fl oz (125 ml) milk
1 beaten egg

Sift the flour and salt, rub in the butter until the mixture resembles breadcrumbs. Stir in the sugar and make a well in the centre, drop in the eggs and gradually add the milk, working in the flour from the sides until the dough is quite smooth and elastic.

Handle the dough lightly, shaping it into small rounds rather than rolling it out, and flattening it with the knuckles to a thickness of ½–¾in (1–2cm). Brush with milk or beaten egg or dust with flour.

Place the scones on greased baking sheets and bake in a very hot oven (425–450°F, 220–235°C; Gas Mark 7–8) for about 10 minutes.

Jumbles

4 oz (125 g) butter
6 oz (175 g) caster sugar
1 egg
Grated rind of 1 lemon
6 oz (175 g) plain flour

Cream the butter and sugar until light and fluffy, beat in the egg and lemon rind and fold in the sifted flour.

Divide the mixture into three portions and roll each into a long sausage shape, about ½in (1cm) wide; cut these into 3–4in (8–10cm) pieces and set in the form of an "S" on greased baking trays. Bake in a moderate oven (325°F, 165°C; Gas Mark 3) for 30 minutes until light brown.

Cornish Splits

These are the authentic vehicles for all that cream and strawberry jam. The splits freeze well. Heat them through in a warm oven before serving. It is important to warm the ingredients before mixing them to ensure a good rise.

1 oz (25 g) fresh yeast
½ teaspoon sugar
¼ pint (150 ml) water
1 oz (25 g) lard
2½ fl oz (75 ml) milk
4 oz (125 g) butter
1½ lb (675 g) plain strong flour
1 teaspoon salt

Cream the yeast with the sugar until smooth. Add the water, warmed to room temperature, and mix in a tablespoon of the flour. Cover with a clean cloth and leave in a warm place, free of draughts, until the mixture is foaming and the yeast working. Combine the lard, milk and butter in a bowl and put into a low oven to warm up to just above blood temperature.

Warm the flour and salt in another bowl to about 100°F, 39°C. Make a well in the centre and pour in the milk, lard and butter mixture and the yeast mixture. Work with the hands until a smooth dough is formed. Turn on to a floured board and knead lightly for 2 minutes. Put in a large well-buttered basin, cover with a clean floured cloth and leave in a warm place until risen to twice its size.

(It is very difficult to know what twice the size means after leaving the dough for some time. I take the precaution of marking the bowl before covering the dough, at the point to which I feel it should rise.)

Turn out the dough on to a floured board and knead lightly until smooth and elastic. Divide into balls about 1in (2½cm) across, press flat to half the height, place on a greased baking sheet, cover again with a floured cloth and leave to rise in a warm place until doubled in size.

Bake the splits in a moderate oven (350°F, 180°C; Gas Mark 4) for about 25 minutes until golden brown on the top.

Remove from the baking sheet on to a wire rack and rub over with a brush dipped in melted butter, or a piece of buttered paper. Serve in a warmed white damask napkin with the top of the napkin folded over the splits.

The hot splits should be split in half, spread with clotted cream and topped with strawberry jam (preferably the home-made variety with lots of lumpy pieces of strawberries in it). If you buy jam, for this purpose get Tiptree or Elsenham; it is worth having a really good jam.

Brandy Snaps with Clotted Cream

8 oz (225 g) plain flour
4 oz (125 g) butter
8 oz (225 g) soft brown sugar
2 eggs, beaten
2 teaspoons brandy

Put the flour in a bowl. Add the butter in small pieces and rub into the flour until the mixture resembles fine breadcrumbs. Add the sugar, eggs and brandy and beat with a wire whisk until the mixture is smooth. Well grease a baking sheet. Drop spoonfuls of the mixture, well spaced, on to the sheet and bake in a hot oven (425°F, 220°C; Gas Mark 7) for about 5 minutes until golden. Remove with a spatula (working as fast as you can), drape over the handle of a wooden spoon, roll up and remove as soon as they become crisp—this will be a matter of seconds.

Leave to cool and fill each end with a dollop of clotted cream.

Rich Devon Cakes

These specialities of Devon are made with clotted cream and therefore extremely rich. They are really more like biscuits than cakes and need no adornment except a dredging of sugar.

Clotted cream, which is almost the same in content as butter, replaces any fat in the recipe.

1 lb (450 g) plain flour
8 oz (225 g) clotted cream
1 egg beaten
8 oz (225 g) caster sugar

Put the flour into a bowl, add the clotted cream and the beaten egg and mix with the fingertips until the mixture resembles fine bread-crumbs. The mixture should be the consistency of shortcrust pastry and therefore reasonably easy to roll out, but if it is too crumbly bind it with a little milk.

Roll out the dough to ⅛in (3mm) thick and cut into circles with a floured 2in (5cm) pastry cutter. Dredge circles generously with caster sugar. Place the rounds on greased baking sheets and bake in a hot oven (400°F, 205°C; Gas Mark 6) for about 15 minutes or until crisp and golden brown.

Macaroons

Makes 24 Macaroons

Rice paper
4 oz (125 g) ground almonds
6 oz (175 g) caster sugar
2 egg whites
1 tablespoon cornflour
Few drops almond essence
2 teaspoons cold water
24 blanched almonds

Reserve 1 tablespoon of the egg white. Combine the ground almonds, sugar and remaining egg whites and mix until smooth with a wooden spoon. Stir in the cornflour, almond essence and water and mix until the ingredients are well blended.

Spoon the mixture into a forcing bag with a ½in (1cm) nozzle and pipe the mixture into large round buttons onto rice paper. Press an almond lightly into the top of each round and brush them with a little beaten egg white.

Bake in a moderately hot oven (375°F, 190°C; Gas Mark 5) for 10–15 minutes until risen, golden brown and slightly cracked on the surface. Remove from the oven and, when they are cool enough to handle cut off surplus rice paper and leave to cool on a wire rack.

Bristol Cake

1 lb (450 g) plain flour
1½ teaspoons baking powder
6 oz (175 g) butter
6 oz (175 g) caster sugar
8 oz (225 g) sultanas
3 eggs

Sift the flour and baking powder, rub   butter and add the sugar and sultanas.

Mix to a dropping consistency with the lightly beaten eggs, spoon into a greased 6–7in (15–18cm) cake tin and bake in a moderate oven. (350°F, 180°C; Gas Mark 4) for 1½–2 hours.

Buttermilk Cake

1 lb (450 g) plain flour
½ teaspoon bicarbonate of
    soda
½ teaspoon each, mixed spice,
    ground ginger and ground
    cinnamon
8 oz (225 g) butter
8 oz (225 g) soft brown sugar
1 lb (450 g) mixed dried fruit
2 oz (50 g) black treacle
2 eggs
½ pt (250 ml) buttermilk or
    sour milk

Sift the flour, bicarbonate of soda and the spices; rub in the butter and add the sugar and dried fruit. Mix with the treacle, lightly beaten eggs and the buttermilk.

Spoon the mixture into a 9–10in (23–25cm) greased cake tin and bake in a moderate oven (350°F, 180°C; Gas Mark 4) for about 2 hours.

Harrier Cake

8 oz (225 g) plain flour
½ teaspoon bicarbonate of
    soda
¾ teaspoon baking powder
1 teaspoon mixed spice
4 oz (125 g) butter
4 oz (125 g) caster sugar
8 oz (225 g) chopped dates
2 oz (50 g) chopped walnuts
1 oz (25 g) treacle or syrup
1 egg
½ pt (250 ml) milk

Sift the flour, bicarbonate of soda, baking powder and spice; rub in the butter and add the sugar. Fold in the dates and walnuts and mix with the treacle, beaten egg and milk.

Spoon the mixture into a greased 6–7in (15–18cm) cake tin and bake in a moderate oven (350°F, 180°C; Gas Mark 4) for 1½–2 hours.

Guard's Cake

1 lb (450 g) plain flour
2 teaspoons mixed spice
1 teaspoon bicarbonate of soda
8 oz (225 g) butter
8 oz (225 g) Demerara sugar
4 oz (125 g) mixed peel
4 oz (125 g) sultanas
5 eggs

Sift the flour, spice and bicarbonate of soda; rub in the butter and add the sugar, mixed peel and sultanas. Mix to a dropping consistency with the beaten eggs; spoon into a greased 9–10in (23–25cm) cake tin and bake in a moderate oven (350°F, 180°C; Gas Mark 4) for about 2 hours.

Almond Cake

1 lb (450 g) butter
1 lb (450 g) caster sugar
9 eggs
1 lb (450 g) plain flour
4 oz (125 g) ground almonds
1 teaspoon almond essence
1 oz (25 g) blanched flaked
   almonds

Cream the butter, cut into pieces, with the sugar until light and fluffy. Beat the eggs in a bowl set over a pan of hot water and gradually whisk into the creamed mixture. Fold in the sifted flour, add the ground almonds and the almond essence and mix to a soft dropping consistency without beating the mixture.

Turn into a lined and greased 9–10in (23–25cm) cake tin; level the top and decorate with the flaked almonds. Bake in a moderate oven (350°F, 180°C; Gas Mark 4) for 2 hours.

Battenburg Cake

4 eggs
8 oz (225 g) butter
8 oz (225 g) caster sugar
8 oz (225 g) plain flour
2 teaspoons baking powder
1 teaspoon vanilla essence
Food colouring
2–4 oz (50–125 g) warmed jam
8 oz (225 g) almond paste

Beat the eggs over a pan of warm water; cream the butter and sugar until light and fluffy and gradually beat in the eggs. Fold in the flour sifted with the baking powder and add the vanilla essence.

Divide the cake mixture into two equal portions and colour one portion pink with a few drops of food colouring.

Line a swiss-roll tin with greaseproof paper and lay a twist of greaseproof paper lengthways in the tin, dividing it into two sections. Fill one section of the tin with the pink mixture and the other with the plain cake mixture. Bake in a moderately hot oven (375°F, 190°C; Gas Mark 5) for about 20 minutes and cool on a cake rack.

Trim the sides of the two sections to the same size. Cut each section in half lengthways and brush the sides of each strip with warmed jam; lay a pink strip next to a plain-coloured strip and press together. Brush the top with jam and cover with the two strips, setting a plain above a pink strip and a pink above a plain.

Roll the almond paste out thinly on a surface sprinkled with sugar, cut to a shape that will fit the whole cake. Brush the cake all over with warm jam, then wrap the almond paste round it, leaving the short ends of the cake uncovered. Seal the join neatly.

Fruit Cake

1 lb (450 g) butter
1 lb (450 g) caster sugar
9 eggs
1 lb (450 g) plain flour
8 oz (225 g) currants
8 oz (225 g) sultanas
8 oz (225 g) raisins
4 oz (125 g) chopped candied
    peel
4 oz (125 g) chopped glacé
    cherries

Cream the butter, cut into small pieces, with the sugar until light and fluffy; whisk the eggs in a bowl set over a pan of hot water and beat into the butter and sugar mixture. Fold in the sifted flour, alternately with the currants, sultanas, raisins, candied peel and glacé cherries.

Spoon the mixture into a double-lined, greased 9–10in (23–25 cm) cake tin; level the top and bake in a moderate oven (350°F, 180°C; Gas Mark 4) for 2 hours.

Madeira Cake

In the 19th century, Madeira wine was traditionally served with this cake, hence the name.

1 lb (450 g) butter
1 lb (450 g) caster sugar
9 eggs
1 lb (450 g) plain flour
1 teaspoon grated lemon rind
2 strips citron peel

Cut the butter into small pieces and cream with the sugar until light and fluffy; beat the eggs in a large bowl set over a pan of hot water. Whisk the eggs into the creamed mixture and fold in the sifted flour and the grated lemon rind.

Turn the cake mixture into a lined and greased 9–10in (23–25 cm) cake tin, smooth the top level and bake in a moderate oven (350°F, 180°C; Gas Mark 4) for 30 minutes; arrange the citron peel, cut into narrow strips, over the top and continue baking for another 1½ hours.

Christmas Cake

1 lb (450 g) butter
1 lb (450 g) soft brown sugar
9 eggs
1¼ lb (575 g) plain flour
½ teaspoon salt
¾ oz (22 g) mixed spice or cin-
    namon
1 lb (450 g) currants
4 oz (125 g) chopped raisins
1 lb (450 g) sultanas
4 oz (125 g) chopped citron peel
4 oz (125 g) chopped mixed
    peel
4 oz (125 g) blanched chopped
    almonds
8 oz (225 g) chopped glacé
    cherries
Grated rind of ½ lemon
2 oz (50 g) black treacle
5 fl oz (125 ml) rum
Vanilla, almond or ratafia ess-
    ence

Cut the butter into small pieces and cream with the sugar until light and fluffy; beat the eggs in a large bowl set over a pan of hot water and whisk into the creamed mixture. Fold in the flour sifted with salt and mixed spice, alternately with the dried fruits, citron and mixed peel, almonds, cherries and lemon rind. Finally, add the treacle, rum and a few drops of essence.

Turn the cake mixture into a double-lined and greased, 12in (30cm) cake tin and level the top making sure no air pockets are left. Tie a couple of layers of brown paper round the sides of the tin and stand it on a double layer of newspaper in the oven and bake in a moderate oven (325°F, 165°C; Gas Mark 3) for 4½–5 hours. If the cake browns on top before the end of cooking time, cover the top with a double layer of greaseproof or brown paper.

Leave the cake to cool completely before decorating it; it will keep for several weeks if stored in foil and an airtight tin. Cover the cake, top and sides, with almond paste or marzipan and leave to set. Spread Royal Icing over the marzipan and pipe on decoration.

Cherry Cake

1 lb (450 g) butter
1 lb (450 g) caster sugar
9 eggs
1 lb (450 g) plain flour
8–12 oz (225–350 g) chopped
 glacé cherries

Cut the butter into small pieces and beat with the sugar until light and fluffy. Beat the eggs in a large bowl set over a pan of hot water; whisk into the butter and sugar mixture and fold in the sifted flour. Add the chopped cherries and turn the mixture into a lined and greased, 9–10in (23–25cm) cake tin.

Smooth the top level and bake in a moderate oven (350°F, 180°C; Gas Mark 4) for 2 hours.

Pound Cake

8 eggs
1 lb (450 g) butter
1 lb (450 g) caster sugar
1 lb (450 g) plain flour
1 lb (450 g) mixed dried fruit
4 oz (125 g) chopped mixed peel
Grated rind of 1 lemon
2 fl oz (50 ml) brandy

Beat the eggs in a deep bowl above a pan of hot water; cream the butter and sugar until fluffy, gradually beat in the eggs and fold in the flour.

Mix in the fruit, peel, lemon rind and brandy and spoon the mixture into a 9in (23cm) square lined tin. Level the top and bake in a moderate oven (350°F, 180°C; Gas Mark 4) for 2 hours. A few halved walnuts may be placed on the top before baking.

Seed Cake

1 lb (450 g) butter
1 lb (450 g) caster sugar
9 eggs
1 lb (450 g) plain flour
1 teaspoon ground cloves
1 teaspoon cinnamon
2 oz (50 g) caraway seeds

Cut the butter into small pieces and cream with the sugar until fluffy; beat the eggs in a bowl set over a pan of hot water and whisk into the butter and sugar mixture. Fold in the flour sifted with the cloves and cinnamon and add the caraway seeds.

Turn the mixture into a lined and greased, 9–10in (23–25cm) cake tin; smooth the top and bake in a moderate oven (350°F, 180°C; Gas Mark 4) for 2 hours.

Sponge Cake

4 eggs
4 oz (125 g) caster sugar
4 oz (125 g) plain flour
Red jam
Icing sugar

Grease two sandwich tins, 6–7in (15–18cm) wide, and dust with flour. Put the eggs and sugar in a warm bowl, set over a pan of hot water and whisk the mixture until light and creamy; it should be stiff enough to leave a trail from the whisk.

Remove the bowl from the heat, sift in half the flour and fold in lightly with a metal spoon. Add the remaining flour in the same way. Spoon the cake mixture immediately into the prepared tins and bake in a moderately hot oven (375°F, 190°C; Gas Mark 5) for 20 minutes.

When cool, sandwich with jam and dust the top with sifted icing sugar.

Marlborough Cake

4 eggs
8 oz (225 g) caster sugar
6 oz (175 g) plain flour
1 oz (25 g) caraway seeds

Grease and flour an 8–9in (20–23cm) round cake tin. Put the eggs and sugar in a warm bowl and set over a pan of hot water. Whisk steadily until creamy and thick enough for the whisk to leave a trail.

Remove the bowl from the heat, fold in half the sifted flour and the caraway seeds; fold in the remaining flour, using a metal spoon in both instances.

Spoon the mixture into the prepared cake tin and bake in a hot oven (425°F, 220°C; Gas Mark 7) for 10 minutes. When cold, cover the top with sifted icing sugar.

Victoria Sandwich

There are numerous variations of this light layer cake, named after Queen Victoria.

2 eggs
4 oz (125 g) butter
4 oz (125 g) caster sugar
4 oz (125 g) plain flour
1 teaspoon baking powder
½ teaspoon vanilla essence
Jam or butter icing
Icing sugar

Beat the eggs in a bowl set over a pan of warm water; cream the butter and sugar until white and fluffy and gradually beat in the eggs. Carefully fold in the flour sifted with the baking powder; stir in the vanilla essence.

Pour the mixture into two lined sandwich tins, 6–7in (15–18cm) wide; level the top and bake in a moderately hot oven (375°F, 190°C; Gas Mark 5) for 20 minutes until golden and firm, yet springy.

Leave to cool on a cake rack, then sandwich the two layers with jam or butter cream icing and dust the top with sifted icing sugar.

Chocolate Sandwich, melt 2 oz (50 g) chocolate or 1 oz (25 g) cocoa powder in a little milk and add before the flour which should be reduced to 3 oz (75 g); fill with chocolate butter cream and coat with chocolate glacé icing.

Orange or Lemon Sandwich, add the grated rind of 1 orange or lemon after folding in the flour; coat with orange or lemon icing and decorate with crystallised orange or lemon slices.

Basic Butter Icing

6 oz (175 g) butter
12 oz (350 g) icing sugar, sieved
3 tablespoons warm water

Cream butter until soft. Gradually add sugar, beating all the time until sugar has been absorbed into the butter. Beat in the water and mix until smooth and shining.

Flavourings

Orange Use orange juice instead of water and mix 1 tablespoon finely grated orange peel into the icing.
Lemon Substitute 2 teaspoons lemon juice for 2 teaspoons of water and mix the grated peel of ½ a lemon into the icing.
Chocolate Melt 3 oz (75 g) plain chocolate in a bowl over hot water and mix the melted chocolate into the icing.
Vanilla Add a few drops of vanilla essence to the butter icing and mix well.

Royal Icing

1½ lb (675 g) icing sugar,
    sieved
3 egg whites
Juice of 1 lemon
Water if necessary

Beat the egg whites and mix in the sugar and lemon, beating well until the mixture is light and thick. This makes enough to cover a 12in (30cm) cake.

Richmond Maids of Honour I

There are several recipes for these classic little curd cakes which, according to one tradition, derived their name from the Maids of Honour attending Queen Elizabeth I at the Palace of Richmond;

yet another tradition claims that the cakes were a favourite delicacy of Anne Boleyn's and her entourage and were given their nickname by Henry VIII.

8 oz (225 g) rich shortcrust pastry
4 oz (125 g) dry curds
3 oz (75 g) butter
2 eggs
2½ fl oz (65 ml) brandy
3 oz (75 g) caster sugar
3 oz (75 g) floury baked
   potatoes
1 oz (25 g) ground almonds
¼ teaspoon grated nutmeg
Grated rind of 1½ lemons
Juice of ½ lemon

Roll the pastry out thinly and use to line 16 patty tins; sieve the curds and mix with the softened butter; beat the eggs with the brandy and sugar and blend into the curd mixture.

Mix the potatoes with the almonds, nutmeg, lemon rind and juice; stir into the curds, mixing well. Fill the lined patty tins and bake until set in a moderate oven (350°F, 180°C; Gas Mark 4).

Richmond Maids of Honour II

The fresh curds in this version are made from 2 pt fresh milk, 2 pt boiling water, lemon juice and 2 beaten eggs.

12 oz (350 g) rich shortcrust pastry
8 oz (225 g) fresh curds
4 egg yolks
8 fl oz (180 ml) clotted cream
Grated rind of 1 lemon
Pinch cinnamon and nutmeg
6 oz (175 g) currants
2 oz (50 g) caster sugar
5 fl oz (125 ml) brandy

Roll out the pastry and line 24 patty tins. Mix the fresh curds with the beaten egg yolks, clotted cream, lemon rind, cinnamon, nutmeg, currants, sugar and brandy. Blend thoroughly, spoon into the patty tins and bake in a moderate oven (350°F, 180°C; Gas Mark 4) for 20–25 minutes.

44

Wimbledon Cake

1 lb (450 g) plain flour
8 oz (225 g) butter
8 oz (225 g) caster sugar
8 oz (225 g) currants
2 oz (50 g) chopped candied
    peel
½ pt (250 ml) sour milk
2 oz (50 g) syrup
1 teaspoon mixed spice
½ teaspoon bicarbonate of
    soda

Sift the flour and rub in the butter; add the sugar, currants and candied peel. Mix the milk with syrup, spice and bicarbonate of soda and blend into the flour mixture.

Spoon into a shallow, 8in square, greased cake tin and bake in a moderate oven (350°F, 180°C; Gas Mark 4) for 2 hours.

Windsor Castle Cake

4 oz (125 g) plain flour
¾ teaspoon baking powder
6 oz (175 g) ground rice
8 oz (225 g) butter
8 oz (225 g) caster sugar
Grated rind of 1 lemon
2 eggs
½ pt (250 ml) milk

Sift the flour and baking powder, mix in the ground rice and rub in the butter. Add the sugar and lemon rind and mix to a dropping consistency with the beaten eggs and the milk.

Spoon into a greased 6–7in cake tin and bake in a moderate oven (350°F, 180°C; Gas Mark 4) for 2 hours.

NURSERY TEAS

Nursery tea 1880 (*Mary Evans Picture Library*)

Gone, sadly, are the days of nurseries hidden behind the green baize door or situated at the very top of the house with a gate to guard the stairs but in Victorian and Edwardian days this afternoon meal was one of great enchantment with the nursery maid preparing the feast and nanny presiding over the teapot. Usually children took lunch with grown-ups and had to be on their best behaviour but at tea-time they could relax away from the frowns of their parents and the reminders to 'sit up straight' and mind their manners.

In the winter there were bread and crumpets to be toasted in front of the fire and in the summer there were sardine sandwiches and sponge cakes filled lavishly with raspberry jam or butter icing. Dolls were treated to a tea-party too, from the miniature sets of china touted round by salesmen for the potteries (hoping also to make a sale to the lady of the house for a proper grown-up sized service) and, in the nursery 'make believe' went hand in hand with Garibaldi biscuits and cream fingers.

Although the green baize doors, nannies and nursery maids have become a thing of the past, the practice of giving children a combined tea and supper still continues with sandwiches, cakes and biscuits forming the main part of the meal.

Sardine Sandwiches

Tinned sardines
Thinly sliced white or brown
   bread
Softened butter
Salt and white pepper

Drain the oil from the sardines and mash the sardines with a fork until smooth. Season with a little salt and if the children are fairly grown up a little white pepper. A little tomato ketchup can also be mixed with the sardines.

Butter the bread, spread slices with sardine paste, cover with second buttered slice, press firmly together and remove crusts. Cut sandwiches into triangles or halves.

Banana and Cream Sandwiches

1 banana
2 tablespoons clotted cream
2 teaspoons sugar
Slices of buttered white bread
   with the crusts removed

Peel and mash the banana and mix in the cream and sugar. Spread the banana mixture on bread, cover with second slice of bread, press firmly together and cut in half.

Chocolate Spread and Hundreds and Thousands Sandwiches

Spread slices of white bread with the crusts removed thickly with chocolate spread, sprinkle with hundreds and thousands, cover with second slices and cut into triangles.

The following sandwiches are more recent in origin and prove popular because of children's inbuilt enjoyment of sweet and savoury combinations:

1   Fill sandwiches with marmalade and then slices of cold well-browned sausages.

2   Fill sandwiches with peanut butter topped with redcurrant jelly.

NOTE: Cheese sandwiches should not be given to children for tea-time as they tend to encourage nightmares.

See also potted meat and fish paste for sandwiches on page 60.

French Toast

Thin slices white bread
2 eggs
½ teaspoon salt
Scant ½ pint (250 ml) milk
Few drops vanilla essence
Cinnamon
2 oz (50 g) butter
Sugar

Remove the crusts from the bread and cut each slice into three fingers.
    Beat the egg with the salt and milk until smooth and flavour with a few drops of vanilla essence. Dip the bread fingers into this mixture. Heat the butter in a heavy frying pan, add the bread slices and fry on both sides until crisp and golden. Drain on kitchen paper and dust lightly with sugar and cinnamon. Serve hot.

Currant Bread

1 lb (450 g) plain flour
3 teaspoons baking powder
½ teaspoon bicarbonate of soda
4 oz (125 g) butter
6 oz (175 g) caster sugar
6 oz (175 g) currants
6 oz (175 g) raisins
1 oz (25 g) candied peel
2 oz (50 g) black treacle
2 eggs
½ pt (250 ml) buttermilk

Sift the flour; add the baking powder and bicarbonate of soda and rub in the butter. Blend in the sugar, currants, raisins and candied peel and mix to a smooth dropping dough with the treacle, beaten eggs and buttermilk.

Spoon this mixture into two greased 1 lb (450 g) loaf tins and bake in a moderate oven (350°F, 180°C; Gas Mark 4) for about 1½ hours.

Teabread

These sweet loaves or breads have a fairly coarse texture and should be eaten within a short time of baking as they do not keep well. They are usually baked in loaf or round cake tins.

1 lb (450 g) plain flour
1 oz (25 g) baking powder
4 oz (125 g) butter
4 oz (125 g) caster sugar
2 eggs (optional)
½ pt (250 ml) milk (approx.)

Sift the flour and baking powder, rub in the butter to a crumbly mixture and add the sugar. Make a well in the centre, drop in the eggs if used and gradually add the milk, stirring with a round-bladed knife until the dough has a soft dropping consistency.

Spoon into one greased 2 lb (900 g) or two 1 lb (450 g) loaf tins and bake in a moderate oven (350°F, 180°C; Gas Mark 4) for 1½ hours.

A number of ingredients, especially fruits, can be added to the basic sweet loaf mixture:

Banana Loaf, add 2 lb (900 g) mashed bananas before the milk.

Date and Apricot Loaf, add 4 oz (125 g) soaked and chopped apricots and 4 oz (125 g) chopped dates to the dry ingredients.

Date and Banana Loaf, blend 4 oz (125 g) chopped dates and 8–12 oz (225–350 g) mashed bananas into the dry mix.

Date and Walnut Loaf, add 2 oz (50 g) chopped walnuts, 4 oz (125 g) chopped dates and ½ teaspoon mixed spice to the dry ingredients.

Orange Loaf, blend 4 oz (125 g) thick orange marmalade and the grated rind of 1 orange into the mixture before adding the milk.

Spice Loaf, add 2 oz (50 g) sultanas, 2 oz (50 g) currants and 1 teaspoon mixed spice into the dry mix.

Syrup and Nut Loaf, blend 3 oz (75 g) chopped nuts and 6 oz (175 g) chopped dates into the dry ingredients; blend 4 oz (125 g) syrup or clear honey with the milk.

Walnut Loaf, add 4 oz (125 g) finely chopped walnuts to the dry ingredients.

Malt Nut Bread

1 lb (450 g) plain flour
1 oz (25 g) baking powder
2 oz (50 g) soft brown sugar
4 oz (125 g) seedless raisins
2 oz (50 g) finely chopped walnuts
2 oz (50 g) black treacle
4 oz (125 g) malt extract
½ pt (250 ml) milk

Sift the flour and baking powder and mix in the sugar, raisins and walnuts.

Blend the treacle and malt extract with the milk, stir into the flour and beat to a smooth dough. Spoon into greased loaf tins and bake in a moderate oven (350°F, 180°C; Gas Mark 4) for about 1½ hours.

Sultana Scones

8 oz (225 g) plain flour
1 teaspoon baking powder
Pinch salt
1½ oz (40 g) butter or
  margarine
1 oz (25 g) caster sugar
2 oz (50 g) sultanas
¼ pint (150ml) sour milk, buttermilk or ½ yoghurt and ½
  water
Milk for glazing

Combine flour and salt and rub in the butter, cut into small pieces, with the fingertips until the mixture resembles fine breadcrumbs. Add the sugar and sultanas and mix well. Gradually mix in the sour milk to make a firm dough. Turn onto a floured board and knead lightly until smooth. Roll out to ½in (1cm) thickness and cut into rounds with a 2in (5cm) pastry cutter.

Place on an ungreased baking sheet, brush with a little milk, and bake in a very hot oven (450°F, 235°C; Gas Mark 8) for 10 minutes until lightly golden. Cool on a wire rack, split and spread with butter or clotted cream.

Muffins

3 lb (1.3 kg) strong plain flour
1 oz (25 g) salt
1 oz (25 g) fresh yeast
½ tablespoon sugar
1½ pt (850 ml) warm water

Sift the flour and salt and mix in the yeast creamed with the sugar and a little of the warm water; knead well and leave to rise until doubled in size.

Knock back and divide the dough into pieces of 2½ oz (65 g) each; shape into rounds, ½in (1cm) thick, on a floured surface to prevent sticking. Bake on greased heated oven plates of iron or steel (425°F, 220°C; Gas Mark 7) for 15–20 minutes. Turn when half baked to cook evenly on both sides. Serve split with butter and jam.

Sally Lunn Buns

Named after Sally Lunn who lived in Bath and used to 'cry' the buns in the streets; legend goes that the cry—in West Country French—was really *Solet Lune* or *Soleilume* with reference to the sun represented on top of the bun and the moon underneath, substantiated in earlier spellings of *Soli Lune, Solielume* or *Sollyluma*.

1 lb (450 g) plain flour
2 teaspoons salt
½ oz (15 g) fresh yeast
½ tablespoon sugar
2 oz (50 g) fat
4 fl oz (100 ml) milk
2 beaten eggs

Sift the flour and salt and add the yeast creamed with the sugar, the fat melted in the warm milk and one beaten egg. Mix to a smooth dough of dropping consistency and leave to rise and double in size.

Knock the dough back and shape to fit greased round baking rings about 6 in (15 cm) wide; leave to rise until the rings are full, then bake in a hot oven (425°F, 220°C; Gas Mark 7) for 15–20 minutes. Brush with beaten egg halfway through baking. Serve hot, filled with whipped cream and sprinkled with crushed sugar.

Apple Gingerbread

2 oz (50 g) butter or lard
2 oz (50 g) caster sugar
1½ oz (40 g) golden syrup
4 oz (125 g) plain flour
1 teaspoon ground ginger
½ teaspoon bicarbonate of soda
½ teaspoon ground cloves
Milk
12 oz (350 g) peeled, cored and
    finely chopped cooking apples

Line and butter a shallow, 8in (20cm) cake tin. Melt the butter, sugar and syrup over gentle heat. Remove from the heat and blend in the sifted flour, ginger, bicarbonate of soda, sugar and cloves. Mix with milk and the apples until the mixture has a soft dropping consistency.

Spoon into the prepared tin and bake in a moderate oven

(350°F, 180°C; Gas Mark 4) for 1½ hours. Cover with cinnamon icing when cool.

Flapjacks

4 oz (125 g) margarine
2 oz (50 g) brown sugar
5 oz (150 g) Golden Syrup
8 oz (225 g) rolled oats
Pinch salt
6 oz (175 g) caster sugar
8 oz (225 g) plain flour
1 oz (25 g) baking powder
4 oz (125 g) oatmeal
3 eggs
½pt (250 ml) milk

Grease and flour a shallow, 8in (20cm) square tin. Melt the margarine, brown sugar and syrup over gentle heat; pour over the rolled oats mixed with a pinch of salt and add the caster sugar. Blend thoroughly, then fold in the flour sifted with the baking powder, and the oatmeal. Mix to a soft dropping consistency with the beaten eggs and the milk.

Spoon the mixture into the prepared tin and bake in a moderately hot oven (375°F, 190°C; Gas Mark 5) for about 40 minutes or until risen and firm. Serve cut into squares or fingers.

Rock Cakes

8 oz (225 g) plain flour
Pinch salt
2 teaspoons baking powder
2 oz (50 g) butter
2 oz (50 g) lard
2 oz (50 g) sultanas
2 oz (50 g) currants
4 oz (125 g) soft brown sugar
Grated rind of ½ lemon
1 egg
2 tablespoons milk

Combine flour, salt and baking powder together in a bowl. Add the fats, cut into small pieces, and rub the fats into the other ingredients, using the fingers, until the mixture resembles fine breadcrumbs. Add the fruit, sugar and lemon rind and mix well. Beat the egg with the milk and mix the liquid into the dry ingredients to make a stiff dough.

Spoon into twelve mounds on a well-greased baking dish and bake in a hot oven (400°F, 205°C; Gas Mark 6) for 15–20 minutes until firm and golden brown. Cool on a wire rack.

Victoria Sandwich Cup Cakes

These little cup cakes are basically made from a Victoria Sandwich cake mixture. Additional ingredients give rise to a number of varieties.

2 eggs
4 oz (125 g) butter
4 oz (125 g) caster sugar
4 oz (125 g) plain flour
1 teaspoon baking powder

Beat the eggs in a bowl set over a pan of warm water; cream the butter and sugar and gradually beat in the eggs. Carefully fold in the flour sifted with the baking powder. Spoon the cake mixture into lined or greased patty tins and bake in a moderately hot oven (375°F, 190°C; Gas Mark 5) for 15 minutes. The cakes may be iced with plain or coloured glacé icing when cool.

From this basic recipe, the following versions can be made, adding the additional ingredients after folding in the flour:

Golden Bettys, fold in 2 teaspoons ground ginger and 2 oz (50 g) melted Golden Syrup.

Madelines, bake the cake mixture in greased dariole moulds; coat when cool with melted red jam and roll in desiccated coconut.

Widecombe Fair Gingerbread

6 oz (175 g) plain flour
1 teaspoon ground ginger
5 oz (150 g) butter
6 oz (175 g) caster sugar
6 oz (175 g) black treacle

Sift the flour, add the ginger and rub in the butter; blend in the sugar. Dissolve the treacle and mix into the flour, blending to a soft consistency.

Drop the mixture in spoonfuls on to greased baking trays and bake in a moderate oven (350°F, 180°C; Gas Mark 4) for 30–40 minutes or until firm, yet springy to the touch.

Rhubarb Gingerbread

2 oz (50 g) butter or lard
2 oz (50 g) caster sugar
1½ oz (40 g) black treacle
4 oz (125 g) plain flour
½ teaspoon bicarbonate of soda
3 teaspoons ground ginger
1 egg
Milk
1¼ lb (575 g) cleaned and chopped rhubarb
6 oz (175 g) chopped crystallised ginger

Line and grease a shallow, square 8in (20cm) cake tin; sprinkle lightly with flour. Melt the butter, sugar and treacle over low heat; add the flour sifted with bicarbonate of soda and 1 teaspoon ground ginger. Stir in the beaten egg and enough milk to give a soft consistency.

Spoon half the gingerbread mixture into the prepared tin, top with the rhubarb and crystallised ginger and sprinkle with the remaining 2 teaspoons of ground ginger. Spoon in the remaining cake mixture and bake in a moderate oven (350°F, 180°C; Gas Mark 4) for 1½ hours.

Honey Cakes

6 oz (175 g) butter
4 oz (125 g) caster sugar
4 oz (125 g) honey
Grated rind of 1 lemon
6 eggs
12 oz (350 g) plain or self-raising flour
1 oz (25 g) ground cinnamon
1 oz (25 g) honey
4 oz (125 g) mixed peel

Cream the butter, sugar and honey until light and fluffy; add the finely grated lemon rind and beat in the eggs, one at a time. Fold in

55

the sifted flour. Mix the last three ingredients together, spread this over the base of greased patty tins and spoon the cake mixture over. Bake in a moderate oven (350°F, 180°C; Gas Mark 4) oven for 20 minutes. Turn out, with the spicy mixture on top.

Alternatively, make up the cake mixture and spoon into a lined and greased 7–8in (18–20cm) cake tin. Bake in a moderate oven (325°F, 165°C; Gas Mark 3) for 1–1½ hours.

Somerset Apple Sauce Cake

4 oz (125 g) butter
8 oz (225 g) brown sugar
1 egg
6 oz (175 g) unsweetened apple
   sauce
8 oz (225 g) self-raising flour
½ teaspoon each, cinnamon,
   cloves, nutmeg and salt
4 oz (125 g) raisins
Vanilla butter icing

Cream the butter and sugar until light and fluffy; gradually beat in the beaten egg and add the apple sauce. Stir in the sifted flour, spices and salt and finally the raisins. Spoon into a greased 8in (20cm) cake tin and bake in a moderate oven (350°F, 180°C; Gas Mark 4) for 1 hour.

When cool cover with vanilla butter icing.

Sultana Cake

1 lb (450 g) butter
1 lb (450 g) caster sugar
9 eggs
1 lb (450 g) plain flour
1–1½ lb (450–675 g) sultanas
4 oz (125 g) chopped candied
   peel
2 oz (50 g) chopped glacé
   cherries
Grated rind of 1 lemon

Cream the softened butter and sugar; whisk the eggs in a bowl set over a pan of hot water and beat into the creamed mixture. Fold in the sifted flour, the sultanas, peel, cherries and lemon rind and mix gently to a soft dropping consistency.

Turn the cake mixture into a lined and greased 9–10in (23–25cm) cake tin, level the top and bake in a moderate oven (350°F, 180°C; Gas Mark 4) for 2 hours.

Savoury Bacon Potato Cakes

1 lb (450 g) potatoes (peeled weight)
2 teaspoons salt
Freshly ground black pepper
2 oz (50 g) butter
3 oz (75 g) flour
2 oz (50 g) bacon rashers with the rinds removed

Cook the potatoes in boiling salted water until tender. Drain well and mash until smooth with the seasoning and butter. Finely chop the bacon and fry over a medium heat, without extra fat, for 5 minutes. Drain off excess fat. Beat the flour into the potato mixture and add the bacon pieces. Cool and then roll out to ¼in (6mm) thickness on a well-floured board. Cut into circles with a floured pastry cutter.

Heat a little bacon fat or lard in a heavy frying pan or a griddle, add the cakes and cook for about 2 minutes on each side until the cakes are golden brown. Serve as quickly as possible.

These cakes go well with soup and I have had a great success by making them about 2in (5cm) in diameter and serving them with the soup course at a dinner party.

Lemon Kali Cake

2 oz (50 g) lard
8 oz (225 g) plain flour
2 oz (50 g) caster sugar
1 oz (25 g) candied peel
½ oz (15 g) lemon kali (sherbert)
1 egg

Rub the lard into the sifted flour, add the sugar, candied chopped peel and lemon kali. Mix to a dropping consistency with the beaten egg and water.

Spoon into a greased 6in cake tin and bake for 30–40 minutes in a moderate oven (350°F, 180°C; Gas Mark 4).

FARMHOUSE TEAS

High tea 1878 (*Mary Evans Picture Library*)

These are family affairs—hearty, lavish spreads to satisfy the appetites of workers coming in from the fields having probably only had bread and cheese for lunch and children coming home hungry from school. The woman of the house presides over a large, brown teapot encased in a hand-knitted tea cosy while the head of the house carves a ham or

58

cold leg of lamb and still, in many rural districts, says a prayer before the family begin to eat. The kitchen table groans beneath the weight of sandwiches, cakes, biscuits, scones and buns and the smell of baking fills the air. This, for many, is the main meal of the day, a time to relax, a 'high' tea with all the trimmings; a good leisurely meal when the highlights of the day are relived and the plans for the next one talked over.

These farmhouse teas can often be shared by those travelling around the countryside at farms that advertise 'cream teas' and farmhouses which offer 'bed and breakfast' to the tourist. Their contents will vary according to the district but in the west you will almost always find clotted cream and home-made jam on the table together with a home-made pasty, scones and, perhaps an egg and bacon pie. The butter might well be home-made too, rich golden in colour and sweet as a buttercup waiting to be spread generously on thick slices of crusty bread, heavy cake or lardy cake.

In Dorset and Devon you may find apple cake appears on the menu together with rich buns and cakes made with local cider and in Cornwall you might well notice that sugar is not stirred into the tea—a hangover from the days of John Wesley, the Cornish Methodist Minister who urged his followers not to put sugar in their tea in order to help boycott the sugar supplies which, in those days, came largely from slave-run plantations in the West Indies.

Potted Pastes

Potted pastes make delicious savoury sandwich fillings. For farmhouse teas they are generously spread between thick slices of freshly baked bread with the crusts left on. Pickles can be served with them. More delicate 'drawing room' sandwiches can be made by spreading the paste more thinly on wafer thin slices of brown or white buttered bread; the crusts should be removed and each sandwich cut into three fingers

Potted Tongue

8 oz (225 g) cooked ox tongue
Pinch nutmeg, ginger, mace
and thyme
1 small clove garlic
6 oz (175 g) butter
Salt and freshly ground black
pepper

Pass half the tongue through the fine blades of a mincing machine.

Combine the spices, thyme and garlic clove in a mortar and pound with a pestle until the thyme is almost powdered and the garlic amalgamated with the other ingredients.

Combine 4 oz (125 g) of butter with the minced tongue and the spice mixture and mix to a smooth paste. Cut the remaining tongue into very small dice and mix it with the paste, seasoning with salt and pepper. Pack in a small dish.

Clarify the remaining butter by bringing it to the boil and straining it through a piece of muslin. Pour the hot butter over the potted tongue and leave to cool.

Potted Shrimps

6 oz (175 g) butter
8 oz (225 g) peeled shrimps or
prawns
Salt and freshly ground black
pepper
¼ teaspoon mace
¼ teaspoon ground nutmeg
Pinch cayenne

Melt 4 oz (125 g) butter. Add shrimps or prawns, season with salt, pepper, mace and nutmeg, cover tightly and stew for 40 minutes over a *low* heat, stirring every now and then to prevent them from browning.

Remove from the heat, strain off the juices and pack the shrimps tightly in a small earthenware jar. Melt remaining 2 oz (50 g) of butter and strain over the shrimps or prawns through a sieve lined with a piece of muslin.

Sprinkle with a little cayenne pepper and chill in a refrigerator.

Potted Salmon

8 oz (225 g) salmon cut off the
   bone and skinned
¼ pint (150 ml) white wine
2½ fl oz (75 ml) water
2 sprigs parsley
1 small onion
1 bay leaf
Salt and freshly ground black pepper
Pinch mace and ground nutmeg
4 oz (125 g) butter

Put the skin and bones of the salmon in a small saucepan with the white wine, water, parsley, onion (peeled and sliced) and the bay leaf. Season with salt and pepper and bring to the boil, cover tightly and cook for ½ hour over a high heat. Strain off the liquid into a clean pan and boil fast until reduced to half the quantity.

Place the salmon in a small earthenware pot. Pour in the reduced liquid, add a little mace and nutmeg, cover with foil so that no air can escape and bake in a moderate oven (350°F, 180°C; Gas Mark 4) for 30 minutes or until the salmon is just tender.

Beat the salmon and juice with 3 oz (75 g) of melted butter until smooth. (Use a wooden spoon, pass through a food mill or purée in a liquidiser.) Check seasoning, adding more if necessary—the salmon should be rather on the highly seasoned side. Press firmly into a small jar and cover with melted butter strained through a piece of muslin.

Ham Paste

If you cook a whole piece of ham or gammon on the bone, this is a useful way to use up those untidy trimmings of ham that remain at the end of the carving. The paste can be served as a first course or used as a sandwich filling.

2 large onions
1 lb (450 g) cooked ham or gammon
6 oz (175 g) butter
¼ pint (150 ml) dry cider
Salt and freshly ground black pepper
Pinch cayenne pepper
¼ teaspoon paprika pepper
Pinch mace and ground nutmeg
Pinch finely chopped sage

Peel and roughly chop the onions. Pass the ham through the coarse blades of a mincing machine. Melt 2 oz (50 g) of butter in a heavy frying pan. Add the onions and cook over a low heat until soft and transparent. Remove from the heat, add the ham, cider and another 2 oz (50 g) of butter, season with salt and pepper, the spices and sage. Mix well and either pound to a paste in a mortar or put in a liquidiser or through a food mill.

Pack into small jars and seal with clarified butter, brought to the boil and strained through a piece of muslin.

Somerset Cottage Loaf

3 lb (1.3 kg) strong plain flour
2 teaspoons salt
1 teaspoon sugar
2 oz (50 g) fresh yeast
3 tablespoons melted butter or
   olive oil
1½ pints (850 ml) blood-warm
   water

Put the flour and salt into a bowl and heat in a low oven until it has reached blood temperature (neither hot nor cold). Cream together the sugar and yeast, add ¼ pint (150 ml) of the warmed water, beat until free from all lumps and leave in a warm place for 5–10 minutes until frothy. Add to the remaining water.

Add the yeast mixture to the flour with the butter or oil and work with the fingers until a smooth dough is formed. Turn on to a floured board and knead until the dough is pliable and elastic. Put into a large greased bowl and cover with a floured cloth. Leave in a warm place until doubled in bulk (about 1 hour).

Turn on to a floured board and knead again until all the air has been punched out for about 3 minutes. Pull off two-thirds of the dough and form into a large round. Press flat and top with remaining one-third of the dough, shaped into a circle about one-third of the diameter of the large piece; press down firmly. Push the handle of a wooden spoon well into the loaf and remove.

Place the loaf on a greased baking sheet, cover with a floured cloth and leave to rise in a warm place until doubled in size— about 40 minutes. Brush with milk and bake in a very hot oven (450°F, 235°C; Gas Mark 8) for 40 minutes or until the bottom of the loaf sounds hollow when tapped.

Teacakes

1 lb (450 g) plain flour
Pinch salt
¼ teaspoon ground cinnamon
2 oz (50 g) butter
½ oz (15 g) fresh yeast *2 tsp:*
3 oz (75 g) caster sugar
3 tablespoons milk
3 oz (75 g) sultanas

Combine the flour, salt and cinnamon in a bowl. Add the butter, cut into small pieces, and rub into the flour with the fingertips until the mixture resembles coarse breadcrumbs. Cream the yeast with the sugar and add the milk, warmed to blood temperature (neither hot nor cold) and mix until smooth. Leave to stand for 5–10 minutes until the mixture becomes frothy on the top.

Make a well in the centre of the flour mixture, pour in the yeast liquid and mix the flour in from the sides of the bowl to make a stiff dough. Put in a large, lightly oiled basin, cover with a floured cloth and leave to stand in a warm place for 1 hour.

Remove the dough from the basin, scatter over the sultanas, turn on to a floured board and knead lightly until they are mixed in. Divide the dough into balls about 2in (5cm) across, form into flat buns, place on a greased baking sheet and leave to rise in a warm place for 30 minutes. Brush with beaten egg and bake in a hot oven (425°F, 220°C; Gas Mark 7) for 15 minutes until golden brown.

Serve hot, split in half and spread with butter.

Westcountry Brack

1 lb (450 g) dried fruit (raisins,
   sultanas, currants)
8 oz (225 g) self-raising flour
1 egg yolk
8 oz (225 g) dark brown sugar
½ pint (250 ml) strained cold
   tea
1 egg
Pinch salt

Soak fruit and sugar overnight in the tea. Mix with rest of ingredients. Put in loaf tin. Bake 1¼ hours in a hot oven (400°F, 205°C; Gas Mark 6). Slice thinly, spread with butter.

Revel Buns

Traditionally made for village festivals, the buns were baked wrapped in sycamore leaves or sometimes shaped and baked as loaves.

1 lb (450 g) plain flour
2 teaspoons salt
Pinch cinnamon
½ oz (15 g) fresh yeast
½ tablespoon sugar
2 oz (50 g) fat
2–3 tablespoons saffron milk
5 fl oz (125 ml) Devon cream
1 egg
6 oz (175 g) currants
Icing sugar

For the saffron milk, dissolve a pinch of saffron in a little milk and leave to soak overnight.

Sift the flour, salt and cinnamon, add the creamed yeast and sugar, and the fat melted in the saffron milk; mix in the cream. Add the beaten egg and mix to a smooth dough.

Knead thoroughly, leave to rise until doubled in size, knock back and add the currants. Shape into small buns and, if possible, bake the buns wrapped in sycamore leaves in a moderately hot oven (375° F, 190° C; Gas Mark 5) for about 35 minutes. Sprinkle the cooled buns with icing sugar.

Easter Buns

8 oz (225 g) plain flour
½ teaspoon mixed spice
¼ teaspoon cinnamon
4 oz (125 g) butter
4 oz (125 g) caster sugar
2 oz (50 g) currants
2 oz (50 g) chopped, candied peel
1 egg, beaten
2 tablespoons brandy

Put the flour into a bowl with the mixed spice and cinnamon and rub in the butter using the fingertips until the mixture resembles coarse breadcrumbs. Mix in the sugar, currants and candied peel.

Mix the egg with the brandy. Add the liquid to the ingredients in the bowl and mix with your hands to a firm dough.

Roll out to ¼in (6mm) thick on a floured board and cut into 2in (5cm) rounds. Place the circles on a greased baking sheet and bake in a moderate oven (350°F, 180°C; Gas Mark 4) for 20 minutes. Slide on to a rack and leave to cool a little before serving, cut in half and spread with butter.

Cornish Fairings

Fairing was originally a gift bought at a fair, but later came to mean a cake or sweet sold at a fair simply because the gingerbread stall was a major feature at them.

1 lb (450 g) flour
½ teaspoon mixed spice
1 teaspoon ground ginger
5 oz (150 g) butter
2 oz (50 g) lard
5 oz (150 g) Demerara sugar
4 oz (125 g) candied citron peel
8 oz (225 g) Golden Syrup
4 level teaspoons bicarbonate of
    soda
4 level teaspoons cream of
    tartar

Sift the flour and add the mixed spice and ginger; rub in the butter and lard and mix in the sugar and peel.

Blend the syrup with the bicarbonate of soda and cream of tartar, add to the flour mixture and mix to a soft paste. Roll out, 1in (2½cm) thick, cut into 1in (2½cm) wide strips and cut these in 1in (2½cm) pieces.

Lift onto baking trays allowing room for spreading. Bake in a moderate oven (350°F, 180°C; Gas Mark 4) for about 30–40 minutes, or when risen and firm.

Clotted Cream

I have been told that clotted cream first came to the West Country, like saffron, via the Phoenicians who came to Cornwall in search of tin. Clotted cream much resembled a thick, creamy, yoghurt-like substance which they had in their own country. Whatever its origin the rich yellow cream of Devon and the slightly thicker, more crusty, clotted cream of Cornwall are famous throughout the country.

Devonshire Clotted Cream

2 quarts (2 litres) Channel Island
  milk or rich, creamy fresh milk

Put the cream into a large enamel bowl that can be put over a flame (or use a flameproof Pyrex dish) and leave it to settle in a cool place for 24 hours until all the cream has risen and settled on the surface.

Put the cream over a *very low heat* and scald until bubbles rise to the surface forming a ring around the top of the pan (this is one of those pieces of cooking magic that it is impossible to describe but you will see the ring, the same size as the bottom of the pan, clearly as it forms.) The length of time this takes depends on the depth of the pan but on no account must the milk be allowed to boil.

Carefully remove the pan from the heat and leave it in a cool place to settle for a further 24 hours.

Use a slotted spoon and carefully skim off the crusty cream from the top of the pan and put it into a bowl. Keep it in a refrigerator until it is required.

Use the buttermilk or skimmed milk from below the cream for baking or for making soups or sauces.

Cornish Clotted Cream

This is sometimes made with whole cream as opposed to creamy milk and the bowl of settled cream or milk is put into a pan of hot water before being scalded. The method takes longer but the cream is thicker and even more rich than the Devonshire product.

A well-heeled and pleasantly eccentric friend of ours brings a large enamel bowl of this solid cream with him on summer picnics (he brings the cream and I bring the food).

Scones made with Cream

1 lb (450 g) plain flour
1 teaspoon salt
1½ teaspoons baking powder
2 oz (50 g) butter
2 eggs
¼ pint (150 ml) single cream
Milk

Sieve the flour into a bowl with the salt and baking powder. Add the butter, cut into small pieces, and rub into the flour with fingertips until the mixture resembles coarse breadcrumbs. Beat the eggs with the cream. Make a well in the centre of the flour and butter mixture, pour in the cream and eggs and mix to a firm dough, adding a little milk if necessary.

Turn the dough on to a floured board and knead lightly until smooth—don't work for longer than is absolutely necessary. Roll out to ¾in (2cm) thick. Cut into 2in (5cm) rounds and bake in a hot oven (400°F, 205°C; Gas Mark 6) for about 15 minutes until risen and lightly browned.

Serve the scones cut in half with strawberry jam and clotted cream.

Savoury Cheese Scones

These are also delicious to serve with a rich vegetable soup in the winter.

8 oz (225 g) self-raising flour
Pinch salt
Pinch cayenne
6 oz (175 g) grated Cheddar
   cheese
4 oz (125 g) butter or margarine
1 small egg, beaten

Put the flour in a bowl with the salt and a little cayenne pepper. Add 4 oz (125 g) cheese and the fat, cut into small pieces, and rub into the flour until the mixture resembles coarse breadcrumbs. Add enough water to make a firm pliable dough and knead on a floured board until just smooth. Roll out, using a well-floured rolling pin, to ½in (1cm) thick and cut into 2in (5cm) circles with a floured pastry cutter.

Brush with beaten egg and sprinkle with remaining grated cheese. Bake in a hot oven (425°F, 220°C; Gas Mark 7) for about 15 minutes until golden brown. Serve the scones warm.

Savoury Scones

1 lb (450 g) plain flour
1 teaspoon bicarbonate of soda
1 teaspoon cream of tartar
1 tablespoon salt
3 oz (75 g) lard
¾ pt (400 ml) buttermilk

Sift the flour, bicarbonate, cream of tartar and salt; rub in the lard and stir to a smooth dough with the buttermilk.

Knead lightly and shape into small, flat rounds, about ½in (1cm) thick. Cook on a hot griddle for about 4 minutes on each side until golden brown, or bake in a hot oven (425–450°F, 220–235°C; Gas Mark 7–8) for about 10 minutes.

Drop Scones

¾ pt (400 ml) milk
2 eggs
5 oz (150 g) sugar
2 oz (50 g) oil or melted butter
1 lb (450 g) plain flour
1 oz (25 g) baking powder
Pinch salt

Beat together the milk, eggs, sugar, oil or melted butter; fold in the flour sifted with baking powder and salt. Mix to a soft dropping consistency.

Drop the batter in spoonfuls on to a heated griddle and cook until bubbles appear on top, then turn and cook on the other side. Serve hot or cold, with butter or cream, and jam.

Devonshire Yeast Cake

1 lb (450 g) plain flour
2 teaspoons salt
2 oz (50 g) fat
½ oz (15 g) fresh yeast
½ tablespoon sugar
1 beaten egg
4 fl oz (100 ml) warm water and
    milk
4 oz (125 g) currants
2 oz (50 g) chopped candied
    lemon peel
½ grated nutmeg

Mix all the ingredients except the dried fruits and spice to an enriched dough; knead thoroughly and set to rise.

Knock the dough back, add the currants, peel and nutmeg and knead again. Shape the dough and place in a greased cake tin. Prove and bake in a very hot oven (450°F, 235°C; Gas Mark 8) for 1 hour. After 15 minutes reduce the temperature to 375°F, 190°C; Gas Mark 5.

Figgie Hobbin

8 oz (225 g) plain flour
¾ teaspoon baking powder
2 oz (50 g) chopped suet
2 oz (50 g) lard
8 oz (225 g) dried chopped figs
2–3 fl oz (50–75 ml) milk

Sift the flour and baking powder, rub in the suet and lard and mix with the chopped figs. Blend in enough milk to give a stiff dough.

Roll the dough out, ½in (1cm) thick, on a floured surface and cut into 4in (10cm) squares. Set on greased baking trays, score the surfaces lightly and bake in a hot oven (400°F, 205°C; Gas Mark 6) for 30 minutes.

Fig Sly Cake

8 oz (225 g) rich shortcrust
   pastry
3 oz (75 g) chopped cooked figs
1½ oz (40 g) chopped walnuts
1 oz (25 g) currants
¾ oz (20 g) raisins
1 oz (25 g) caster sugar

Roll the pastry out into two thin rounds. Mix the figs, walnuts, currants and raisins with the sugar and arrange this mixture over one pastry round. Moisten the edges, cover with the other pastry round and seal the edges firmly.

Set on a greased baking tray; brush the top with a sugar and water glaze and bake in a hot oven (425°F, 220°C; Gas Mark 7) for about 20 minutes.

Cornish Heavy Cake

1 lb (450 g) plain flour
Pinch salt
1 lb (450 g) butter
6 oz (175 g) currants
Milk

Sift the flour and salt; divide the butter into four equal parts and rub one quarter into the flour until the mixture has a crumbly texture. Add the currants and enough cold water to give an elastic dough. Knead lightly and roll out to an oblong shape.

Dot two thirds of the pastry with another quarter of butter; fold in the pastry, turn and roll out again. Repeat the process of dotting with butter, folding, turning and rolling out twice more until all the butter is used up.

Roll the pastry out to a rectangle, 1in (2½cm) thick, score the surface in a diamond pattern and brush with milk. Bake in a very hot oven (450°F, 235°C; Gas Mark 8) for 30 minutes reducing the temperature after 10 minutes to 400°F, 205°C; Gas Mark 6.

Old English Cider Cake

2 eggs
4 oz (125 g) butter
4 oz (125 g) caster sugar
8 oz (225 g) plain flour
1 teaspoon baking powder
½ grated nutmeg
5 fl oz (125 ml) cider

Beat the eggs over a pan of warm water; cream the butter and sugar until fluffy and gradually beat in eggs. Fold in the flour sifted with the baking powder and add the nutmeg and cider.

Spoon the cake mixture in a 9in (23cm) sandwich tin lined with greaseproof paper and bake in a moderately hot oven (375°F, 190°C; Gas Mark 5) for 20 minutes.

Cornish Black Cake

12 oz (350 g) butter
12 oz (350 g) caster sugar
12 eggs
8 oz (225 g) plain flour
¾ teaspoon baking powder
½ teaspoon bicarbonate of soda
1 teaspoon mixed spice
1 teaspoon grated nutmeg
2 teaspoons ground cinnamon
8 oz (225 g) rice flour
2 lb (900 g) currants
4 oz (125 g) chopped raisins
12 oz (350 g) chopped sultanas
8 oz (225 g) candied orange peel
8 oz (225 g) candied lemon peel
8 oz (225 g) blanched chopped almonds
2 tablespoons brandy

Cream the butter and sugar until fluffy; beat the eggs in a large bowl over a pan of hot water until creamy. Whisk eggs into creamed mixture then fold in the sieved flour, baking powder, bicarbonate of soda, mixed spice, nutmeg, cinnamon and rice flour. Add the currants, raisins, sultanas, orange and lemon peel, almonds and lastly the brandy.

Turn into double-lined and greased 9in (23cm) cake tins, level the tops and bake in a moderate oven (350°F, 180°C; Gas Mark 4) for 3 hours. One cake is traditionally stored for a whole year and eaten on the anniversary of being baked.

Cover the cake completely with marzipan and decorate with glacé or Royal icing.

The North Devon Black Cake is similar, but also includes 6 oz (175 g) black treacle.

Devon Potato Cake

6 oz (175 g) plain flour
½ teaspoon mixed spice
1 teaspoon baking powder
2 oz (50 g) butter
6 oz (175 g) mashed potatoes
4 oz (125 g) brown sugar
8 oz (225 g) currants
½ oz (15 g) caraway seeds
2 eggs

Sift the flour with the mixed spice and baking powder; rub in the butter and add the potatoes, sugar, currants and caraway seeds.

Add the beaten eggs and mix well; pour into a well-greased shallow cake tin and bake in a hot oven (400°F, 205°C; Gas Mark 6) for 30 minutes. Serve hot, cut into squares.

A Penzance Cake

1 lb (450 g) plain flour
½ teaspoon bicarbonate of soda
4 oz (125 g) butter
2 teaspoons cinnamon
1 lb (450 g) currants
8 oz (225 g) chopped crystal-
    lised ginger
4 oz (125 g) mixed chopped peel
2 eggs
5 fl oz (125 ml) warm milk

Sift the flour and bicarbonate of soda, rub in the butter and add the cinnamon, currants, crystallised ginger and peel. Mix to a soft dough with the beaten eggs and the milk.

Spoon into a greased 9–10in (23–25cm) cake tin and bake in a moderate oven (350°F, 180°C; Gas Mark 4) for 2 hours.

Dripping Cake

1 lb (450 g) plain flour
1 teaspoon grated nutmeg
1 teaspoon bicarbonate of soda
8 oz (225 g) dripping
8 oz (225 g) soft brown sugar
4 oz (125 g) currants
4 oz (125 g) sultanas
2 oz (50 g) mixed peel
4 eggs
2–3 tablespoons milk

Sift the flour, nutmeg and bicarbonate of soda; rub in the dripping and add the sugar, currants, sultanas and peel.

Mix to a dropping consistency with the beaten eggs and milk; spoon into a 9–10in (23–25cm) cake tin lined with buttered greaseproof paper. Bake in a moderate oven until firm (350°F, 180°C; Gas Mark 4), approximately 1½–1¾ hours.

Devonshire Apple Cake

The Dorset Apple Cake is similar, but also includes 2 oz (50 g) currants and 1 oz (25 g) mixed peel; the top is sprinkled with brown sugar rather than granulated.

8 oz (225 g) self-raising flour
1 teaspoon salt
4 oz (125 g) butter
4 oz (125 g) caster sugar
1 lb (450 g) peeled, cored and
    sliced cooking apples
2 eggs
1 oz (25 g) granulated sugar

Mix the flour and salt, rub in the butter, and add the caster sugar and apples. Gather the mixture with the lightly beaten eggs and spoon into two greased 8–9in (20–23cm) sandwich tins; sprinkle with granulated sugar and bake in a hot oven (400°F, 205°C; Gas Mark 6) for 30–40 minutes.

Strawberry Shortcake

8 oz (225 g) flour
4 oz (125 g) caster sugar
2 teaspoonsful baking powder
1 lb (450 g) strawberries
4 oz (125 g) butter
½ teaspoonful salt
Little milk
Devonshire cream

Sieve together flour, baking powder and salt, rub in the butter until the mixture resembles coarse meal. Add very gradually enough milk to give the mixture the consistency of a soft dough, working the liquid in with a knife. Toss the dough on to a floured board and divide into two round flat cakes, one for each sandwich tin. Bake in a hot oven (425°F, 220°C; Gas Mark 7) for 15 minutes. Prepare filling. Wash and hull strawberries and put aside sufficient number for decoration on top of cake. Mash the rest with a silver fork. Add caster sugar, leave until sugar is dissolved. Place half filling on one cake layer, place second layer on top and cover this with rest of filling. Decorate with whole strawberries. Pour juice round cake. Serve with Devonshire cream.

Honiton Apple Cake

1 lb (450 g) firm cooking apples
1 tablespoon water
1 teaspoon cinnamon
4 oz (125 g) dark brown sugar
2 eggs
4 oz (125 g) butter
2 oz (50 g) currants
1 tablespoon finely grated
    lemon rind
1½ oz (40 g) cornflour
4 oz (125 g) fresh fine white
    breadcrumbs
Caster sugar

Peel and core the apples and cut them into chunks. Combine the apples, water, cinnamon and sugar in a saucepan, bring to the boil, cover and simmer until the apples are really soft—about 20 minutes.

Purée the apples through a sieve or a food mill. Separate the eggs and beat the yolks; add the melted butter, currants, apple purée and lemon rind.

Whip the egg whites until stiff and fold in the sifted cornflour (sifting is important with cornflour although it is no longer necessary with plain or self-raising flour). Mix in the breadcrumbs and apple purée mixture as lightly as you can to incorporate them (use a figure of eight movement with a wooden spoon).

Well butter an 8in (20cm) cake tin and dredge it with flour. Spoon in the mixture and cook for 40 minutes in a moderate oven (350°F, 180°C; Gas Mark 4). Leave to cool in the tin, turn out and dredge with a generous amount of caster sugar.

Cider Cake

8 oz (225 g) plain flour
Pinch nutmeg
½ teaspoon ground ginger
½ teaspoon bicarbonate of
   soda
4 oz (125 g) butter
4 oz (125 g) caster sugar
2 eggs
¼ pint (150 ml) medium dry
   cider

Combine the flour in a bowl with the spices and bicarbonate of soda. Mix really well.

Combine the butter and sugar in a bowl and beat until smooth, creamy and light. Beat the eggs and gradually add to the butter mixture, continuing to beat until the ingredients are smooth. Fold in half the flour mixture. Beat the cider until frothy, add it to the mixture, mix lightly and then fold in remaining flour.

Spoon the mixture into a lightly greased shallow cake tin and bake in a moderate oven (325°F, 165°C; Gas Mark 3) for 45 minutes.

Leave in an airtight tin for at least 24 hours before eating.

Honiton Potato Cakes

6 oz (175 g) flour
Pinch salt
5 oz (150 g) lard or clear dripping
1 lb (450 g) mashed potatoes
2 oz (50 g) caster sugar
2 oz (50 g) currants
1 small egg, beaten

Combine the flour and salt in a bowl. Add the lard or dripping and rub it in with fingertips until the mixture resembles coarse breadcrumbs. Add the potato, sugar and currants and mix well. Add the egg and mix to a firm dough, adding a little milk if necessary.

Roll out the dough to ¾in (2cm) thickness on a floured board and cut into circles 2in (5cm) across. Bake the cakes in a hot oven (400°F, 205°C; Gas Mark 6) for about 10 minutes until cooked through and light golden in colour.

Note: The cakes can also be fried in a little clean dripping or lard until golden on both sides.

Rum Gingerbread

Keep this pale amber ginger cake in a sealed tin or polythene container for three to four days before eating to allow it to absorb moisture and develop its flavour.

8 oz (225 g) plain flour
Pinch salt
½ teaspoon ground cinnamon
1 teaspoon ground ginger
3 oz (75 g) butter
2 oz (50 g) soft brown sugar
2 tablespoons Golden Syrup
¼ pint (150 ml) milk and water
1 teaspoon bicarbonate of soda
1 oz (25 g) split, blanched almonds
2 tablespoons dark rum

Combine the flour, salt, cinnamon and ginger in a bowl and mix well. Combine the butter, sugar, Golden Syrup, milk and water in a saucepan and heat slowly until the butter and sugar has melted. Make a well in the centre of the flour, pour in the liquid and mix well until smooth. Dissolve the bicarbonate of soda in 1 tablespoon of water, pour the mixture into the cake mix and stir really well to incorporate all the ingredients.

Spoon into a well-greased tin about 10in (25cm) square and bake in a moderate oven (325°F, 165°C; Gas Mark 3) for 1 hour. Scatter over the almonds and continue to bake for a further 10 minutes. Leave to cool in the tin before turning out.

Turn out, prick all over with a skewer and pour over the rum.

Saffron Yeast Cake

A traditional Cornish cake still to be found on many tea-tables these days, especially in farmhouses, and sold in most bakers. The cake is more like a bread really and is usually served with the slices spread with butter.

2 tablespoons boiling water
½ small teaspoon strand
    saffron
1 oz (25 g) fresh yeast
1 teaspoon sugar
¼ pint (150 ml) milk
1 lb (450 g) plain flour
1 teaspoon salt
2 oz (50 g) butter
2 oz (50 g) lard
2 oz (50 g) caster sugar
4 oz (125 g) currants
2 oz (50 g) mixed peel

Pour the boiling water over the saffron and leave it to steep for an hour.

Cream the yeast with the sugar, add the milk (warmed to blood temperature—neither hot nor cold) and mix well. Leave to stand in a warm place until frothing—about 10 minutes.

Put the flour into a bowl with the salt. Add the butter and lard, cut into small pieces, and rub into the flour until the mixture resembles coarse breadcrumbs. Add the caster sugar, currants and mixed peel and mix well. Add the yeast mixture and the strained saffron water and mix to a soft dough. Turn on to a floured board and knead until smooth. Put in a greased bowl, cover with a clean cloth dusted with flour and leave to rise in a warm place until doubled in bulk (about 1 hour). Knock the air out of the dough and put it in a well-greased loaf tin.

Bake in a hot oven (400°F, 205°C; Gas Mark 6) for 10 minutes, then lower the temperature to moderate (350°F, 180°C; Gas Mark 4) and continue to cook for a further 30 minutes. Cool in the tin.

Lardy Cakes

Also known as Shaley or Sharley Cake, this was traditionally served at tea-time on Saturdays and Sundays.

76

1 lb (450 g) plain flour
½ tablespoon salt
½ oz (15 g) fresh yeast
½ tablespoon sugar
½ pt (250 ml) warm water
12–14 oz (350–400 g) lard
2 oz (50 g) crushed lump sugar
¼ teaspoon each, nutmeg, cinnamon and allspice
1 oz (25 g) currants and sultanas

Make a plain dough by mixing the sifted flour and salt with the yeast creamed with sugar and water. Knead until smooth, then set aside until doubled in size. Knock back.

Roll the dough out to a rectangular shape, ½in (1cm) thick. Dot with one third of the lard, 1½in (4cm) apart, and sprinkle with a third of the sugar. Fold the dough in three as for flaky pastry; fold once more from the side, turn and roll out from the open end.

Repeat the process of dotting with lard and sugar twice more and at the last rolling out, sprinkle with sugar, spices, currants and sultanas.

Roll out to the size of a square baking tin. Mark the top into squares along which the baked bread will be broken, never cut. Bake in a hot oven (425°F, 220°C; Gas Mark 7) for 15–20 minutes.

Pitchy Cake

The name arises from 'pitching' fat, currants and sugar into the bread dough.

1½ lb (675 g) plain flour
½ tablespoon salt
½ oz (15 g) fresh yeast
½ tablespoon sugar
¾ pt (400 ml) warm water
8 oz (225 ml) fat
4 oz (125 g) currants
4 oz (125 g) sugar

Make a plain bread dough by sifting the flour with salt and mixing it until smooth with the creamed yeast and sugar, and the warm water. Knead well and leave to rise.

Knock the dough back, work in (pitch in) the fat, cut into small pieces, the currants and sugar. Knead again, shape into a loaf and set in a greased baking tin to prove. Bake in a hot oven (425°F, 220°C; Gas Mark 7) for 1½ hours. Serve with butter or cream, and jam.

Ruthven Cake

1 lb (450 g) plain flour
2 teaspoons salt
½ teaspoon ground cinnamon
½ oz (15 g) fresh yeast
3 oz (75 g) caster sugar
Grated rind of 1 lemon
4 oz (125 g) butter
2½ fl oz (65 ml) milk
2 eggs

Sift the flour, salt and cinnamon, add the yeast creamed with the sugar and blend in the lemon rind. Mix to a smooth dough with the butter melted in the warm milk and adding the beaten eggs. Knead lightly and leave to rise.

Knock the dough back, set in a greased cake tin and prove before baking in a hot oven (400°F, 205°C; Gas Mark 6) for 1 hour.

Fochabers Gingerbread

8 oz (225 g) butter
4 oz (125 g) caster sugar
8 oz (225 g) black treacle
1 pt (500 ml) beer
1 lb (225 g) plain flour
½ teaspoon bicarbonate of
    soda
2 teaspoons each, ground
    ginger and mixed spice
1 teaspoon each, ground cinna-
    mon and cloves
4 oz (125 g) sultanas
4 oz (125 g) currants
3 oz (75 g) finely chopped can-
    died peel
3 oz (75 g) ground almonds

Line and grease a round, 10in wide, shallow cake tin; sprinkle lightly with flour.

Cream the butter and sugar until light and fluffy; dissolve the treacle in the beer and sift the flour, bicarbonate of soda and the spices. Fold the flour into the creamed mixture, alternately with the treacle and beer; add the sultanas, currants, candied peel and ground almonds.

Pour into the prepared tin and bake for about 3 hours in a moderate oven (350°F, 180°C; Gas Mark 4).

Portree Plum Cake

This cake improves with keeping and can be stored in an airtight tin for at least one week.

1 lb (450 g) plain flour
1 oz (25 g) baking powder
8 oz (225 g) butter
1 teaspoon each, ground cinna-
    mon and grated nutmeg
8 oz (225 g) Demerara sugar
4 oz (125 g) chopped candied
    peel
1 lb (450 g) currants
3 eggs
½ pt (250 ml) stout

Sift the flour and baking powder; rub in the butter and add the spices, sugar, peel and currants. Mix to a dropping consistency with the beaten eggs and the stout.

Spoon into a greased 9–10in cake tin and bake in a moderate oven (350°F, 180°C; Gas Mark 4) for 2 hours.

Cuddieston Cake

12 oz (350 g) butter
12 oz (350 g) caster sugar
6 eggs
1½ lb (675 g) plain flour
¾ teaspoon baking powder
1 lb (450 g) sultanas
1 lb (450 g) currants
8 oz (225 g) chopped glacé
    cherries
8 oz (225 g) chopped mixed peel
4 oz (125 g) ground almonds
2 oz (50g) golden syrup
5 fl oz (125 ml) milk

Cut the butter into small pieces and beat with the sugar until light and creamy. Whisk the eggs in a bowl over a pan of hot water and beat into the butter and sugar: fold in the flour sifted with the baking powder, adding this alternately with the sultanas, currants, cherries and peel. Stir in the almonds, syrup and enough milk to give a dropping consistency.

Spoon the cake mixture into a double-lined and greased 9–10in cake tin; smooth the top and tie brown paper round the tin before baking in a moderate oven (325°F, 165°C; Gas Mark 3).

Simnel Cake

4–5 eggs
8 oz (225 g) butter
8 oz (225 g) caster sugar
8 oz (225 g) plain flour
1 teaspoon each, grated
   nutmeg, cinnamon
    and allspice
¾ teaspoon salt
8–12 oz (225–350 g) sultanas
4 oz (125 g) chopped candied
   peel
1 lb (450 g) currants
2 oz (50 g) black treacle
1½ lb (675 g) marzipan
Apricot jam
1 egg yolk
Olive oil

Beat the eggs in a bowl over a pan of warm water; cream the butter and sugar until fluffy and light; gradually beat in the eggs and fold in the flour, spices and salt. Add the sultanas, peel, currants and treacle and mix well.

Line an 8in (20cm) round cake tin with greaseproof paper. Roll a third of the marzipan into a circle to fit the tin. Put half the cake mixture in the tin, level and cover with the marzipan circle. Cover with the remaining cake mixture, level the top and bake in a moderate oven (325°F, 165°C; Gas Mark 3) for 3½ hours.

When cool, roll out the remaining marzipan to fit the top of the cake. Brush the top with jam and cover with the marzipan, press down and mark the top into 1in (2½cm) squares. Make small balls from the marzipan trimmings and place round the edges.

Brush the top with egg yolk beaten with a little oil and put under a medium hot grill to brown lightly.

Lancashire Cakes

1 lb (450 g) plain flour
1 teaspoon salt
½ oz (15 g) lard
½ oz (15 g) fresh yeast
½ tablespoon sugar
½ pt (250 ml) water
4–6 oz (125–175 g) currants
Nutmeg
Sugar
2 oz (50 g) candied peel

Sift the flour and salt, rub in the lard and add the yeast creamed with the sugar and a little warm water; mix to a smooth dough with the remaining water and knead well. Leave the dough to rise and double in size. Knock back.

Roll the dough out to circles the size of a tea plate and sprinkle the centre of each with currants, nutmeg, sugar and peel. Bring in the edges and seal. Turn the rounds over, join underneath, and roll out re-shaping into rounds. Prick well on top, prove and bake in a hot oven (425°F, 205°C; Gas Mark 7) for 15 minutes.

Suffolk Fourses Cake

A traditional bread served to harvesters in the afternoon, together with sweetened beer.

3 lb (1.4 kg) plain flour
1 tablespoon salt
2 teaspoons mixed spice
12 oz (350 g) lard
1 oz (25 g) yeast
½ tablespoon sugar
1½ pt (750 ml) warm water
12 oz (350 g) currants

Sift the flour, salt and spice, rub in the lard and add the yeast creamed with the sugar and a little warm water; add the remaining water and mix to an elastic dough.

Knead thoroughly, set aside to rise until doubled in size. Knock the dough back and knead in the currants. Shape into loaves and set in greased 1 lb loaf tins. Prove and bake in a hot oven (400°F, 205°C; Gas Mark 6) for 45 minutes.

OTHER TEAS

Apart from everyday tea there were special occasions when the serving of afternoon tea was an important and indeed essential part of the ceremonial.

Perhaps most remembered, and indeed often still held, are the dolorous funeral teas when the craft of baking, the cutting of sandwiches and the making of a reviving 'cuppa' reach an apogee of the hostess's art. The lengthy preparations for such repasts often distract the bereaved from unhappy thoughts and the quality of the ham or the lightness of a Victoria sponge provide opportunities for conversation which carefully avoids the reason why everyone has met.

But there were teas for more happy occasions—in particular those put on to add to the enjoyment of summer sports. The tennis tea was an essential part of country life, as were croquet and cricket teas. Those served at Henley, Hurlingham, the Eton and Harrow match and, later, Wimbledon, were an essential part of the London season. Tea still survives at such sporting events. Though the quality of the food may not be quite so fine, the special delight of strawberries and cream served in the tea interval is still as enjoyable as ever.

A remarkable survival of more leisured days are the Buckingham Palace garden party teas, which give an opportunity for the Royal Family to meet deserving British and overseas citizens in an atmosphere closely resembling the rituals established by Victorian society. Indeed, the cucumber sandwiches served in the palace marquees are as good as ever and still provided by a catering company which is a direct descendant of Lyons Corner Houses.

Throughout the year there were weekly 'At Home' teas, not to be confused with the grander and less frequently held afternoon 'At Homes', when there was usually a musical entertainment of some kind. Guests or hosts provided free entertainment except in more affluent households, when professional musicians or singers were employed. The weekly 'At Home' was a more intimate affair, when the servants were sent away and the gentlemen handed round the food. The hostess presided over the teamaking equipage and, for some reason, plates were not handed out.

Formal 'At Homes' were much grander and the food was laid up as a buffet in the dining room and presided over by servants. So successful was this form of entertainment that it became fashionable to celebrate weddings in this way, with the addition of suitable beverages. The Wedding Tea is still more popular than the Wedding Breakfast which was *de rigeur* in the eighteenth and early nineteenth centuries.

In the innovative 1920s, Mrs Beeton's *Household Management* was recommending Bridge Teas, which 'afford a very pleasant afternoon', with the added caveat: 'These generally commence about 3.30pm; punctuality is naturally most essential.'

The lower classes, who were unlikely to be invited to 'At Homes' or to join royalty at tea, indulged their patriotic fervour in street tea parties which still recur for Coronations and Jubilees. Political hostesses, presiding graciously behind formidably polished urns, sugared voters with street and other afternoon entertainments. Just after the turn of the century, the great Liberal, Lady Wimborne, wooed the supporters of an aspiring parliamentarian with such lavish musical teas that their cost became part of a scandal which resulted in a by-election being called.

The emancipation of women led to the Tea Dance—a particular phenomenon of the 1920s which lasted in one form or another until the early sixties. For the first time, women could be seen alone in public and the Tea Dance provided a perfect opportunity to get out of the house in the afternoons and to meet friends over a cup of tea. Restaurants, department stores and hotels were quick to cash in and Tea Dances became a tremendous craze with fierce competition to attract business. Tango Tea, Hungarian Teas, Charleston Teas reflected passing fads, and musicians were dressed to match the decor and dance demonstrations were given. Victor Sylvester began his long career demonstrating the Tango at Harrods.

Nor were Tea Dances always such innocent affairs: They often provided the only opportunity for women to meet and have contact with men, especially in the passionate embrace of a correctly executed tango! Dance-instructors, often Gigolos, moved in to make as much as they could from the bored and lonely women who flocked to the Tea Dances.

But it is the Tennis Tea which most evokes the spirit of those sunny past days. Mrs Beaton, as ever the arbiter, says: 'The meal is informal and usually served out of doors. Iced tea, coffee, claret cup, etc, are served with sandwiches, pastry, cakes and other light viands. The tables are set under shady trees and members of the family or servants are in attendance at them, the visitors themselves going to the tables for what they want.'

The mention of 'claret cup' reminds us that many such jolly occasions were livened up by the discreet introduction of ostensibly 'cooling' or thirst-quenching 'cups'. French hostesses, more worldly-wise as ever, offered the addition of cognac as an alternative to cream or lemon in tea. In England the use of alcohol at tea-time tended to be disguised by euphemisms, probably to counteract the feelings of guilt stirred up by the militant Temperance Societies, whose 'Temperance Teas' were enjoyed by those who supported the campaign amongst the lower classes against the demon drink.

CUPS AND OTHER DRINKS

Badminton Cup

1 bottle of red Burgundy
2 bottles of soda-water
The rind of 1 orange
The juice of 2 oranges
A few thin slices of cucumber
A dessertspoonful of caster sugar
1 wineglassful of Curaçoa

Place all these ingredients, except the soda-water, in a large jug embedded in ice for at least 1 hour, keeping the jug covered. When ready to serve strain into a glass jug, add a few fresh slices of cucumber, and the soda-water.

Champagne Cup

1 bottle of champagne
1 liqueur glass of brandy
2 bottles of soda-water
½ a teaspoonful of Maraschino
A few fine strips of lemon-peel

When the time permits it is much better to ice the liquor which forms the basis of a 'cooling cup' than to reduce the temperature by adding crushed ice. Place the champagne and soda-water in a deep vessel, surround them with ice, cover them with a wet cloth, and let them remain for 1 hour. When ready to serve, put the strips of lemon-rind into a large glass jug, add the Maraschino and liqueur brandy, pour in the soda-water, and serve at once. A teaspoonful of caster sugar may be added.

Claret Cup

1 bottle of claret
1 wine glassful of sherry
1 liqueur glass of brandy
1 liqueur glass of noyeau
1 liqueur glass of Maraschino
The thin rind of 1 lemon
2 or 3 sprigs of balm, borage or
    verbena when procurable
Caster sugar to taste
1 large bottle of soda-water

Put the claret, lemon rind, and 1 or 2 tablespoonfuls of caster sugar into a large jug, cover, and let it stand embedded in ice for 1 hour. Add the rest of the ingredients, and serve. A few strips of cucumber peel may be used instead of balm, borage or verbena.

Claret Cup (Alternative Method)

1 bottle of claret
1 bottle of soda-water
2 glasses of Curaçoa
1 desertspoonful of caster
    sugar, or to taste, a
    few thin strips of lemon rind,
A few thin strips of cucumber rind

Put the claret into a glass jug, add the lemon rind and the cucumber rind, cover, and let the jug stand embedded in ice for 1 hour. Before serving, add the Curaçoa, and the soda-water, and sweeten to taste.

Loving Cup

1 bottle of champagne
½ a bottle of Madeira
¼ (150 ml) of French brandy
1½ pts (750 ml) of water
4 oz (125 g) of loaf sugar
2 lemons
A few leaves of balm
2 or 3 sprigs of borage
    or mint

Rub the peel off 1 lemon with some lumps of sugar, then remove every particle of pith, also the rind and pith of the other lemon, and slice them thinly. Put the balm, borage, the sliced lemons and all the sugar into a jug, add the water, Madeira and brandy, cover, surround with ice, and let the mixture remain thus for about 1 hour. Also surround the champagne with ice, and add it to the rest of the ingredients when ready to serve.

Currant Water

1 lb (450 g) of red currants
8 oz (225 g) of raspberries
1 lb (450 g) caster sugar
2½ pts (2 l) of cold water

Remove the stalks, crush the fruit well with a wooden spoon, then put it into a preserving pan with ½ pt (250 ml) of water, and half the sugar. Stir occasionally until it reaches boiling-point, then strain through muslin or a fine hair sieve. Dissolve the rest of the sugar in a little cold water, boil to a syrup, add it to the fruit syrup, and stir in the remainder of the water. Allow it to stand until quite cold, then serve.

Lemonade, Egg

1 egg
1 dessertspoonful of lemon-juice
1 teaspoonful of caster sugar
    or to taste, nutmeg, cold
    water, ice

Break the egg into a glass, beat it slightly, then add the lemon-juice, sugar, 1 tablespoonful of crushed ice and a little cold water. Shake well until sufficiently cooled, then strain into another glass, fill up with iced water, sprinkle a little nutmeg on the top, and serve.

Cider Cup

1 pt (500 ml) cider
1 lemon
½ pt (250 ml) water
Sprigs of mint
8 oz (225 g) loaf sugar
½ glass sherry
Soda-water to taste
1 red-cheeked apple

Dissolve sugar in the water over a hotplate. Add thinly peeled lemon rind, then bring to the boil. Strain into a jug. Chill in refrigerator or on ice. Add cider and strained lemon juice. Chill. Stir in sherry and about 1 pint chilled soda-water. Add sliced apple and a sprig or two of mint. Place 2 tablespoons crushed ice in the bottom of tall glasses when serving.

Sparkling Cider Cup

1 bottle sparkling cider
2 oz (225 g) loaf sugar
1 small glass brandy
1 small glass curaçao
1 pt (500 ml) tea
Juice of 2 oranges
1 lemon
Fruit in season

Strain off 1 pint of freshly infused China tea on to the sugar. When dissolved, chill in refrigerator or on ice. Chill cider. When required, strain orange juice into tea. Add brandy and curaçao. Pour into a jug. Add slices of lemon, cider, a handful of fresh strawberries or grapes, or a sliced banana.

Fruit Cup

2 pts (1.25 l) ginger ale
Juice of 3 lemons
1 small bottle maraschino cherries
1 tin grated pineapple
Juice of 3 oranges
Sugar to sweeten

Strain lemon and orange juice into a jug. Add cherries and pineapple. Taste. If not sweet enough, add caster sugar to taste. Chill till sugar is dissolved. Add chilled ginger ale or add ginger ale without chilling and cracked ice to taste. Garnish cup with sprigs of borage or mint.

Lemonade

6 large lemons
1 cup caster sugar
2½ pts (1.75 l) water

88

Halve lemons. Extract and strain juice into a jug. Add sugar and water. Stir occasionally until dissolved. Fill tall glasses one-third full of crushed ice. Fill up with lemonade. Float a slice of lemon on top. If wanted sparkling, substitute aerated water for half the water.

Orangeade for Six Persons

Juice of ½ lemon
4 to 6 tablespoons caster sugar
Juice of 4 oranges
Crushed ice
Water

Dissolve sugar to taste in enough boiling water to cover it. Strain in orange and lemon juice. Add 1½ cups crushed ice and 3½ cups cold water or aerated water. Stir until the ice is dissolved. Serve with a slice of orange or lemon or a few strawberries.

Tennis Cup

1 cup cold tea
1 small cup caster sugar
½ cup shredded pineapple
3 sprigs fresh mint
2 pts (1.25 l) stoned cherries
1 orange
2 lemons
2 pts (1.25 l) chilled soda water

Place cherries in a large jug. Add tea, pineapple, sugar, mint, and washed and dried lemon, thinly sliced. Chill for 4 hours in a refrigerator. When required, add the soda water and ice cubes or crushed ice to taste.

JAMS

Basic Preparation and Cooking Method

1 lb (450 g) fruit
1 lb (450 g) sugar
Water

Prepare the fruit according to kind; put in a preserving pan and add water and any other liquid if indicated.

Simmer gently until quite tender; the time varies according to the type of fruit used. Remove the pan from the heat, add the sugar, stir until dissolved and return the pan to the heat.

Boil rapidly, stirring frequently to prevent sticking. Skim when necessary. Test for setting; pot, cover and store.

Testing for Setting

Temperature test. Using a sugar thermometer, a set will be obtained when the temperature reaches between 220–2°F, 104–5°C. This depends on pectin, acid and sugar content.

Saucer test. Put a little jam on a cold saucer and allow to cool. Push the finger across the top of the jam, and the surface will wrinkle when a set has been obtained.

Potting

Jars must be clean and warm. Jelly should be potted at once, jam should be cooled and stirred to prevent the fruit from rising to the top. Fill the pots to the rim as the jam shrinks a little on cooling.

Covering

Wipe the pots, cover the jam with a waxed disc, wax side down, and make sure that it lies flat and no air bubbles are trapped beneath. Cover with damped cellophane, held in place with a rubber band; label when cold with the name and the date. Store in a cool, dry place away from light.

Recipes

The following jam recipes list ingredients in correct proportions; they are all made according to the basic jam method unless otherwise stated.

Apple and Ginger Jam

4 lb (1.8 kg) peeled, cored and sliced cooking apples
Rind and juice of 2 lemons
4 oz (100 g) finely chopped crystallised ginger

1 pt (500 ml) water
3 lb (1.4 kg) preserving sugar

Apple and Pineapple Jam

6 lb (2.8 kg) peeled, cored and sliced cooking apples
6 lb (2.8 kg) preserving sugar
Juice of 2 lemons

1 tin pineapple chunks
2 pt (1.25 l) tinned pineapple juice

Apricot Jam (Fresh)

6 lb (2.8 kg) fresh, stoned apricots

6 lb (2.8 kg) preserving sugar
1 pt (500 ml) water

Follow the basic jam method, placing the stones in a muslin bag and cooking them with the fruit; remove the bag before adding the sugar.

Apricot Jam (Dried)

2 lb (900 g) finely chopped, dried apricots

6 lb (2.8 kg) preserving sugar
6 pt (3.75 l) water

Follow the basic jam method, soaking the apricots in water overnight before chopping them.

Apricot and Tangerine Jam

2 lb (900 g) soaked, finely chopped, dried apricots
7 lb (3.2 kg) preserving sugar

Juice and finely shredded rind of 12 tangerines

Follow the basic jam method, adding the tangerine pips in a muslin bag for the preliminary boiling process.

Blackberry or Bramble Jam

2 lb (900 g) blackberries
2 lb (900 g) preserving sugar
2 tablespoons water
Juice of 1 small lemon

Devonshire Jam

2 lb (900 g) blackberries
2 lb (900 g) elderberries
3 lb (1.4 kg) preserving sugar

Follow the basic jam method, stripping the elderberries from the stalks.

Black Currant Jam

4 lb (1.8 kg) stripped blackcur-
rants
6 lb (2.8 kg) preserving sugar
3 pt (1.75 l) water

Cherry Jam

3 lb (1.4 kg) stoned cherries
3 lb (1.4 kg) preserving sugar
½ pt (250 ml) raspberry juice
1 pt (500 ml) red currant juice

Tie the stones in a muslin bag and boil with the cherries and juices before adding the sugar. Follow the basic jam method.

Cherry and Red Currant Jam

2 lb (900 g) stoned dark
cherries
1 lb (450 g) stripped red cur-
rants
¼ pt (150 ml) water
3 lb (1.4 kg) preserving sugar

Follow the basic jam method; tie the stones in a muslin bag and simmer with the fruit.

Cherry and Gooseberry Jam

3 lb (1.4 kg) stoned cherries
1½ lb (675 g) topped and
tailed gooseberries
1 teaspoon cream of tartar
4 lb (1.8 kg) preserving
sugar

Follow the basic jam method; tie the stones in a muslin bag and simmer with the fruit.

Kentish Cherry Jam

1 lb (450 g) stoned Morello
cherries
1 pt (500 ml) gooseberry or
apple juice
1½ lb (675 g) preserving
sugar

92

Tie the stones in a muslin bag and simmer with the fruit; follow the basic jam method, adding the fruit juice at the beginning.

Damson Jam

5 lb (2.3 kg) stoned damsons   1½ pt (750 ml) water
6 lb (2.8 kg) preserving sugar

Follow the basic jam method, simmering the stones in a muslin bag with the fruit.

Gooseberry Jam

6 lb (2.8 kg) slightly unripe   6 lb (2.8 kg) preserving sugar
   gooseberries   2 pt (1.25 l) water

Follow the basic jam method. For additional flavour, tie 3–4 elder-flower heads per 1 lb (450 g) fruit in muslin and boil with the fruit.

Marrow and Pineapple Jam

4 lb (1.8 kg) peeled marrow   1 large tin of chopped pine-
3 lb (1.4 kg) preserving sugar   apple chunks

Cut the marrow into 1in cubes and soak overnight in the sugar; follow the basic jam method, adding the pineapple chunks and juice.

Pear and Ginger Jam

4 lb (1.8 kg) hard, peeled,   2 oz (50 g) chopped crystallised
   cored and finely chopped   ginger
   pears   Juice of 2 lemons
3 lb (1.4 kg) preserving sugar

Soak the prepared pears with the sugar and lemon juice overnight. Continue as for the basic jam method, adding the ginger.

Pear and Peach Jam

1½ lb (675 g) firm, ripe pears,   Grated rind and juice of 3
   peeled, cored and cubed   lemons
1½ lb (675 g) peaches, skinned,   3 lb (1.4 kg) preserving sugar
   stoned and sliced   ¼ pt (150 ml) water

Autumn Jam

2 lb (900 g) peeled, cored and
sliced cooking apples
2 lb (900 g) peeled, cored and
sliced cooking pears
1½ lb (675 g) peeled, cored and

sliced quinces
Juice and rind of 1 lemon
6 lb (2.8 kg) preserving sugar
1 pt (500 ml) water

Put the peel and cores of the fruit in a muslin bag with the lemon rind and add when boiling up the fruit. Continue as for the basic jam method.

Plum Jam

4 lb (1.8 kg) stoned plums
4 lb (1.8 kg) preserving sugar

½ pt (250 ml) water

Follow the basic jam method, adding the stones in a muslin bag when boiling the fruit.

Raspberry Jam

6 lb (2.8 kg) raspberries

6 lb (2.8 kg) preserving sugar

Use very dry, under-ripe rather than over-ripe fruit; dry the sugar in a cool oven and then follow the basic jam method.

Raspberry and Red Currant Jam

1½ lb (675 g) raspberries
1½ lb (675 g) stripped red currants

3 lb (1.4 kg) preserving sugar
1 pt (500 ml) water

Rhubarb Jam

8 lb (3.6 kg) finely chopped rhubarb
Juice of 4 lemons or 1¼ pt (650

ml) red currant or gooseberry juice
6 lb (2.8 kg) preserving sugar

Rhubarb and Ginger Jam

6 lb (2.8 kg) finely chopped rhubarb
12 oz (350 g) finely chopped,

crystallised ginger
Rind of 1 lemon
5 lb (2.3 kg) preserving sugar

Soak the prepared rhubarb in the sugar for 24 hours. Boil the ginger and lemon in the strained rhubarb syrup for 30 minutes. Add the rhubarb and finish as for basic jam method. Leave for 30 minutes before potting.

INDEX

96